Publisher 2007: Advanced

Instructor's Edition

THOMSON

COURSE TECHNOLOGY

Australia • Canada • Mexico • Singapore
Spain • United Kingdom • United States

Publisher 2007: Advanced

VP and GM, Training Group:	Michael Springer
Series Product Managers:	Charles G. Blum and Adam A. Wilcox
Writer:	Chris Hale
Developmental Editor:	Brandon Heffernan
Copyeditor:	Robert Tillett
Keytester:	Cliff Coryea
Series Designer:	Adam A. Wilcox
Cover Designer:	Abby Scholz

For more information contact:

Course Technology
25 Thomson Place
Boston, MA 02210

Or find us on the Web at: www.course.com

For permission to use material from this text or product, submit a request online at: www.thomsonrights.com

Any additional questions about permissions can be submitted by e-mail to: thomsonrights@thomson.com

Trademarks

Course ILT is a trademark of Course Technology.

Some of the product names and company names used in this book have been used for identification purposes only and may be trademarks or registered trademarks of their respective manufacturers and sellers.

Disclaimer

Course Technology reserves the right to revise this publication and make changes from time to time in its content without notice.

ISBN 10: 1-4239-5129-8
ISBN 13: 978-1-4239-5129-2

Printed in the United States of America

1 2 3 4 5 6 7 8 9 GLOB 09 08 07

Contents

Introduction   **iii**

Topic A: About the manual...iv

Topic B: Setting student expectations ix

Topic C: Classroom setup..xii

Topic D: Support..xvi

Basic design options   **1-1**

Topic A: Publication setup...1-2

Topic B: Custom colors..1-11

Topic C: The Content Library 1-18

Topic D: The Graphics Manager pane 1-23

Unit summary: Basic design options..1-27

Typography   **2-1**

Topic A: Styles and font schemes..2-2

Topic B: Graphics in typography..2-14

Topic C: Precise spacing control 2-24

Topic D: Symbols and special characters 2-29

Unit summary: Typography 2-33

Long publications   **3-1**

Topic A: Sections..3-2

Topic B: Bookmarks...3-6

Unit summary: Long publications...3-9

Mail merge   **4-1**

Topic A: Recipient lists 4-2

Topic B: Mailing labels 4-5

Topic C: The Mail Merge pane..4-6

Topic D: Mail merge fields..4-11

Topic E: Merged publications 4-14

Unit summary: Mail merge 4-17

Interactive forms   **5-1**

Topic A: Web forms 5-2

Topic B: Form settings 5-14

Unit summary: Interactive forms 5-21

Web site publishing   **6-1**

Topic A: Web elements 6-2

Topic B: Web page options 6-14

Topic C: Web site publishing 6-16

Unit summary: Web site publishing...6-19

Course summary   **S-1**

Topic A: Course summary S-2

Topic B: Continued learning after class S-3

Quick reference   **Q-1**

Glossary   **G-1**

Index   **I-1**

Introduction

After reading this introduction, you will know how to:

A Use Course Technology ILT manuals in general.

B Use prerequisites, a target student description, course objectives, and a skills inventory to properly set students' expectations for the course.

C Set up a classroom to teach this course.

D Get support for setting up and teaching this course.

Topic A: About the manual

Course Technology ILT philosophy

Our goal at Course Technology is to make you, the instructor, as successful as possible. To that end, our manuals facilitate students' learning by providing structured interaction with the software itself. While we provide text to help you explain difficult concepts, the hands-on activities are the focus of our courses. Leading the students through these activities will teach the skills and concepts effectively.

We believe strongly in the instructor-led class. For many students, having a thinking, feeling instructor in front of them will always be the most comfortable way to learn. Because the students' focus should be on you, our manuals are designed and written to facilitate your interaction with the students, and not to call attention to manuals themselves.

We believe in the basic approach of setting expectations, then teaching, and providing summary and review afterwards. For this reason, lessons begin with objectives and end with summaries. We also provide overall course objectives and a course summary to provide both an introduction to and closure on the entire course.

Our goal is your success. We encourage your feedback in helping us to continually improve our manuals to meet your needs.

Manual components

The manuals contain these major components:

- Table of contents
- Introduction
- Units
- Course summary
- Quick reference
- Glossary
- Index

Each element is described below.

Table of contents

The table of contents acts as a learning roadmap for you and the students.

Introduction

The introduction contains information about our training philosophy and our manual components, features, and conventions. It contains target student, prerequisite, objective, and setup information for the specific course. Finally, the introduction contains support information.

Units

Units are the largest structural component of the actual course content. A unit begins with a title page that lists objectives for each major subdivision, or topic, within the unit. Within each topic, conceptual and explanatory information alternates with hands-on activities. Units conclude with a summary comprising one paragraph for each topic, and an independent practice activity that gives students an opportunity to practice the skills they've learned.

The conceptual information takes the form of text paragraphs, exhibits, lists, and tables. The activities are structured in two columns, one telling students what to do, the other providing explanations, descriptions, and graphics. Throughout a unit, instructor notes are found in the left margin.

Course summary

This section provides a text summary of the entire course. It is useful for providing closure at the end of the course. The course summary also indicates the next course in this series, if there is one, and lists additional resources students might find useful as they continue to learn about the software.

Quick reference

The quick reference is an at-a-glance job aid summarizing some of the more common features of the software.

Glossary

The glossary provides definitions for all of the key terms used in this course.

Index

The index at the end of this manual makes it easy for you and your students to find information about a particular software component, feature, or concept.

Manual conventions

We've tried to keep the number of elements and the types of formatting to a minimum in the manuals. We think this aids in clarity and makes the manuals more classically elegant looking. But there are some conventions and icons you should know about.

Instructor note/icon

Item	Description
Italic text	In conceptual text, indicates a new term or feature.
Bold text	In unit summaries, indicates a key term or concept. In an independent practice activity, indicates an explicit item that you select, choose, or type.
`Code font`	Indicates code or syntax.
`Longer strings of ▶ code will look ▶ like this.`	In the hands-on activities, any code that's too long to fit on a single line is divided into segments by one or more continuation characters (▶). This code should be entered as a continuous string of text.
	In the left margin, provide tips, hints, and warnings for the instructor.
Select **bold item**	In the left column of hands-on activities, bold sans-serif text indicates an explicit item that you select, choose, or type.
Keycaps like (↵ ENTER)	Indicate a key on the keyboard you must press.
	Warnings prepare instructors for potential classroom management problems.
	Tips give extra information the instructor can share with students.
	Setup notes provide a realistic business context for instructors to share with students, or indicate additional setup steps required for the current activity.
	Projector notes indicate that there is a PowerPoint slide for the adjacent content.

Instructor notes.

Warning icon.

Tip icon.

Setup icon.

Projector icon.

Hands-on activities

The hands-on activities are the most important parts of our manuals. They are divided into two primary columns. The "Here's how" column gives short directions to the students. The "Here's why" column provides explanations, graphics, and clarifications. To the left, instructor notes provide tips, warnings, setups, and other information for the instructor only. Here's a sample:

Do it!

A-1: Creating a commission formula

Here's how	**Here's why**
1 Open Sales	This is an oversimplified sales compensation worksheet. It shows sales totals, commissions, and incentives for five sales reps.
2 Observe the contents of cell F4	F4 ▼ = =E4*C_Rate
	The commission rate formulas use the name "C_Rate" instead of a value for the commission rate.

Take the time to make sure your students understand this worksheet. We'll be here a while.

For these activities, we have provided a collection of data files designed to help students learn each skill in a real-world business context. As students work through the activities, they will modify and update these files. Of course, students might make a mistake and therefore want to re-key the activity starting from scratch. To make it easy to start over, students will rename each data file at the end of the first activity in which the file is modified. Our convention for renaming files is to add the word "My" to the beginning of the file name. In the above activity, for example, students are using a file called "Sales" for the first time. At the end of this activity, they would save the file as "My sales," thus leaving the "Sales" file unchanged. If students make mistakes, they can start over using the original "Sales" file.

In some activities, however, it might not be practical to rename the data file. Such exceptions are indicated with an instructor note. If students want to retry one of these activities, you will need to provide a fresh copy of the original data file.

PowerPoint presentations

Each unit in this course has an accompanying PowerPoint presentation. These slide shows are designed to support your classroom instruction while providing students with a visual focus. Each presentation begins with a list of unit objectives and ends with a unit summary slide. We strongly recommend that you run these presentations from the instructor's station as you teach this course. A copy of PowerPoint Viewer is included, so it is not necessary to have PowerPoint installed on your computer.

The Course ILT PowerPoint add-in

The CD also contains a PowerPoint add-in that enables you to do two things:

- Create slide notes for the class
- Display a control panel for the Flash movies embedded in the presentations

To load the PowerPoint add-in:

1 Copy the Course_ILT.ppa file to a convenient location on your hard drive.
2 Start PowerPoint.
3 Choose Tools, Macro, Security to open the Security dialog box. On the Security Level tab, select Medium (if necessary), and then click OK.
4 Choose Tools, Add-Ins to open the Add-Ins dialog box. Then, click Add New.
5 Browse to and double-click the Course_ILT.ppa file, and then click OK. A message box will appear, warning you that macros can contain viruses.
6 Click Enable Macros. The Course_ILT add-in should now appear in the Available Add-Ins list (in the Add-Ins dialog box). The "x" in front of Course_ILT indicates that the add-in is loaded.
7 Click Close to close the Add-Ins dialog box.

After you complete this procedure, a new toolbar will be available at the top of the PowerPoint window. This toolbar contains a single button labeled "Create SlideNotes." Click this button to generate slide-notes files in both text (.txt) and Excel (.xls) format. By default, these files will be saved to the folder that contains the presentation. If the PowerPoint file is on a CD-ROM or in some other location to which the slide-notes files cannot be saved, you will be prompted to save the presentation to your hard drive and try again.

When you run a presentation and come to a slide that contains a Flash movie, you will see a small control panel in the lower-left corner of the screen. You can use this panel to start, stop, and rewind the movie, or to play it again.

Topic B: Setting student expectations

Properly setting students' expectations is essential to your success. This topic will help you do that by providing:

- Prerequisites for this course
- A description of the target student
- A list of the objectives for the course
- A skills assessment for the course

Course prerequisites

Students taking this course should be familiar with personal computers and the use of a keyboard and a mouse. Furthermore, this course assumes that students have completed the *Publisher 2007: Basic* course or have equivalent experience.

Target student

The target student for this course is an individual who wants to learn about the advanced features of Publisher 2007 and use them to adjust the layout and design of a publication, work with advanced typography, create a publication with sections, perform a mail merge, create interactive forms, and design and publish Web sites.

Course objectives

You should share these overall course objectives with your students at the beginning of the day. This will give the students an idea about what to expect, and it will help you identify students who might be misplaced. Students are considered misplaced when they lack the prerequisite knowledge or when they already know most of the subject matter to be covered.

After completing this course, students will know how to:

- Create a brochure, create a business information set, change the color scheme for a publication, create tint swatches and gradients, use the Content Library to add and insert items, and use the Graphics Manager pane to link and replace pictures.

- Work with styles, change a font scheme, create WordArt objects, create a type mask, wrap text around an image, snap text to a baseline guide, distribute text horizontally, and insert symbols and special characters.

- Create sections in a publication, apply section page numbers, and insert and use bookmarks.

- Create a recipient list for a mail merge, prepare mailing labels, connect to a recipient list, sort and filter a recipient list, add mail merge fields to a publication, and create a merged publication.

- Apply a Web template, insert form input fields, set form properties, and label form elements.

- Preview a Web publication in a browser, convert a print publication to a Web publication, check for common Web page errors and omissions, add alternative text to an image, create hyperlinks, insert a navigation bar, apply a site description and keywords, and publish a Web site from within Publisher.

Skills inventory

Use the following form to gauge students' skill levels entering the class (students have copies in the introductions of their student manuals). For each skill listed, have students rate their familiarity from 1 to 5, with five being the most familiar. Emphasize that this is not a test. Rather, it is intended to provide students with an idea of where they're starting from at the beginning of class. If a student is wholly unfamiliar with all the skills, he or she might not be ready for the class. A student who seems to understand all of the skills, on the other hand, might need to move on to the next course in the series.

Skill	1	2	3	4	5
Creating a brochure					
Creating a business information set					
Changing the color scheme					
Creating tint swatches					
Creating gradients					
Working with the Content Library					
Linking a picture					
Replacing a picture					
Working with styles					
Changing font schemes					
Working with WordArt objects					
Creating a type mask					
Wrapping text around a picture					
Snapping text to a baseline guide					
Distributing text horizontally					
Inserting symbols and special characters					
Creating sections in a publication					
Applying section page numbers					
Creating bookmarks					
Creating a recipient list					
Sorting and filtering recipients					
Adding mail merge fields to a publication					

Skill	1	2	3	4	5
Completing a mail merge					
Inserting form elements					
Sending form data via e-mail					
Labeling form elements					
Converting to a Web publication					
Adding alternative text to a picture					
Creating a hyperlink					
Inserting a navigation bar					
Setting Web page options					
Publishing a Web site					

Topic C: Classroom setup

All our courses assume that each student has a personal computer to use during the class. Our hands-on approach to learning requires they do. This topic gives information on how to set up the classroom to teach this course. It includes minimum requirements for the students' personal computers, setup information for the first time you teach the class, and setup information for each time that you teach after the first time you set up the classroom.

Hardware requirements

Each student's personal computer should have:

- A keyboard and a mouse
- Pentium 500 MHz or higher
- 512 MB RAM
- 2 GB of available hard drive space
- A CD-ROM drive
- An SVGA or higher resolution monitor set to a minimum of 1024 × 768

Software requirements

You will need the following software:

- Windows XP Service Pack (SP) 2, Windows Server 2003, or Windows Vista
- Microsoft Publisher 2007

Network requirements

The following network components and connectivity are also required for this course:

- Internet access, for the following purposes:
  - Downloading the latest critical updates and service packs from www.windowsupdate.com
  - Downloading the Student Data files from www.courseilt.com (if necessary)

First-time setup instructions

The first time you teach this course, you will need to perform the following steps to set up each student computer.

1 Install Windows XP on an NTFS partition according to the software manufacturer's instructions. If the student machines have Internet access, and they are behind a software or hardware firewall, install the latest critical updates and service packs from www.windowsupdate.com.

   Note: You can also use Windows Server 2003, although the screen shots in this course were taken using Windows XP, so students' screens might look somewhat different.

2 From the Control Panel, open the Display Properties dialog box and apply the following settings:

   • Theme—Windows XP

   • Screen resolution—1024 × 768 pixels

   • Color quality—High (24 bit) or higher

3 Display file extensions.

   a Start Windows Explorer.

   b Choose Tools, Folder Options, and select the View tab.

   c Clear the check box for Hide extensions for known file types.

   d Close Windows Explorer.

4 Install Microsoft Office 2007 according to the software manufacturer's instructions, as follows:

   a When prompted for the CD key, enter the code included with your software.

   b Select the Customize installation option and click Next.

   c Activate the Installation Options tab.

   d For Publisher, Office Shared Features, and Office Tools, click the drop-down arrow and choose Run all from My Computer.

   e Set all other options to Not Available.

   f Click Install Now.

   g On the last screen of the Office 2007 installer, click Go to Office Online. Internet Explorer displays the Office Online Web site, and the installer window closes.

   h On the Office Online Web page, activate the Downloads tab.

   i Download and install any available updates.

   j Close Internet Explorer.

5   Start Microsoft Office Publisher 2007. Then, do the following:

    a   Activate the software. After activation, the Welcome to the 2007 Microsoft Office System dialog box appears.

    b   On the Privacy Options screen, verify that "Search Microsoft Office Online for Help content when I'm connected to the Internet" is checked.

    c   Verify that "Download a file periodically that helps determine system problems" is cleared.

    d   Verify that "Sign up for the Customer Experience Improvement Program" is cleared.

    e   Click Next.

    f   Select "I don't want to use Microsoft Update".

    g   Click Finish to close the dialog box, and close Publisher.

6   If necessary, download and install Internet Explorer 7 at http://www.microsoft.com/windows/ie. Accept all defaults during installation.

7   If you don't have the data CD that came with this manual, download the Student Data files for the course. You can download the data directly to student machines, to a central location on your own network, or to a disk.

    a   Connect to www.courseilt.com/instructor_tools.html.

    b   Click the link for Microsoft Publisher to display a page of course listings, and then click the link for Publisher 2007: Advanced.

    c   Click the link for downloading the Student Data files, and follow the instructions that appear on your screen.

Setup instructions for every class

Every time you teach this course (including the first time), you will need to perform the following steps to set up each student computer.

1   If necessary, reset any defaults that have been changed in previous classes.

2   Delete the contents of the Student Data folder, if necessary. (If this is the first time you are teaching the course, create a folder named Student Data at the root of the hard drive. For a standard hard drive setup, this will be C:\Student Data.)

3   Copy the data files to the Student Data folder. (See the download instructions in the preceding section.)

CertBlaster software

CertBlaster pre- and post-assessment software is available for this course. To download and install this free software, students should complete the following steps:

1 Go to www.courseilt.com/certblaster.
2 Click the link for Publisher 2007.
3 Save the .EXE file to a folder on your hard drive. (Note: If you skip this step, the CertBlaster software will not install correctly.)
4 Click Start and choose Run.
5 Click Browse and then navigate to the folder that contains the .EXE file.
6 Select the .EXE file and click Open.
7 Click OK and follow the on-screen instructions. When prompted for the password, enter **c_pub07**.

Topic D: Support

Your success is our primary concern. If you need help setting up this class or teaching a particular unit, topic, or activity, please don't hesitate to get in touch with us. Please have the name of the course available when you call, and be as specific as possible about the kind of help you need.

Phone support

You can call for support 24 hours a day at (888) 672-7500. If you do not connect to a live operator, you can leave a message, and we pledge to return your call within 24 hours (except on Saturday and Sunday).

Web-based support

The Course ILT Web site provides several instructor's tools for each course, including course outlines and answers to frequently asked questions. To download these files, go to www.courseilt.com/instructor_tools.html. For additional Course ILT resources, including our online catalog and contact information, go to http://www.course.com/ilt.

Unit 1

Basic design options

Unit time: 75 minutes

Complete this unit, and you'll know how to:

A Set up a brochure and create a business information set.

B Change the color scheme for a publication, create tint swatches, and create gradients.

C Add items to the Content Library and insert Content Library items into a publication.

D Use the Graphics Manager pane to link and replace pictures.

Topic A: Publication setup

Explanation

After you've learned the basics of working with Publisher, you'll begin to discover ways to make your workflow more efficient. The way in which you set up your publications at the outset will affect how you can work with them once you've started adding content. For example, if you want to create a brochure, you can use a template to establish its layout and color scheme, and then apply content to it.

Templates

Publisher provides several templates for common types of publications. For example, you can select from several preformatted brochure templates that contain placeholders for text and graphics. You can also choose a color and font scheme, select which business information you want to include, and select layout options and other features.

To create a preformatted brochure:

1   Start with a blank publication.

2   In the Format Publication pane, under Quick Publication Options, click Change Template. The Change Template dialog box opens.

3   In the leftmost panel, select Brochures to show the brochure templates.

4   To create a preformatted publication, select a design from either the Newer Designs or the Classic Designs category.

Tell students that they will learn about color schemes, font schemes, business information, mail merge, and forms in later activities.

5   Under Customize, select a color scheme, font scheme, and business information set, if desired.

6   From the Page size list, select 4-panel (3-panel is the default page size).

7   To include a text box for a customer address, check Include customer address.

8   To include a preformatted form, select an option from the Form list.

9   Click OK.

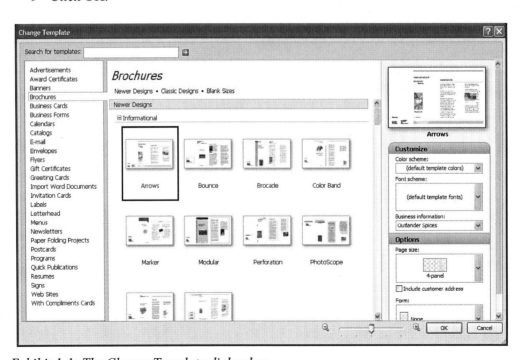

Exhibit 1-1: The Change Template dialog box

Do it!

A-1: Examining a brochure

Here's how	Here's why
If the Publication Types window appears, tell students to close it. Then, in the Options dialog box, clear Show Publication Types when starting Publisher.	
1 Start Publisher 2007	
2 Create a new, blank publication	If necessary.
3 In the Format Publication pane, click **Change Template**	(Under Quick Publication Options.) To open the Change Template dialog box.
In the leftmost panel, click **Brochures**	To view the available brochure templates. You can choose a template with placeholder text and pictures, or a blank template.
4 Select the Bounce template	
Observe the panel to the right	In this panel, you can customize the template with a color scheme or a font scheme, give the brochure three or four panels, include a text box for a customer address, and include a form.
5 Explore a few other brochure templates	To get a feel for the available pre-set layout options and styles.
6 In the center panel, select the Arrows template	
Under Options, from the Page size list, select **4-panel**	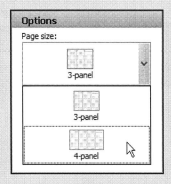
Click **OK**	Publisher asks if you want to apply the template to the current publication, or create a new publication. You'll create a new one.
Click **OK**	The brochure uses Legal-sized paper (14in x 8.5in, or 84pi x 51pi). It has two pages, to form a two-sided publication. Each page has column guides to create four panels, and the margin guides are set to zero. Publisher creates placeholders for the company address and logo, and several text boxes and picture frames.
7 Press (CTRL) + (W)	To close the publication and return to the blank default publication. When prompted to save your changes, click No.

Brochure setup

Explanation

Using a preformatted template can save you time. However, if you want to create your own design and layout from scratch, you can start with a blank publication. By default, Publisher creates a blank, 51 x 66pi (or 8.5 x 11") publication. To change the page size:

1. In the Format Publication pane, under Quick Publication Options, click Change Page Size to open the Page Setup dialog box, shown in Exhibit 1-2.
2. Select a page size from one of the categories. (The first category is Standard.)
3. Under Page, edit the page's width and height, if necessary.
4. Under Margin Guides, edit the page margins, if necessary.
5. Click OK.

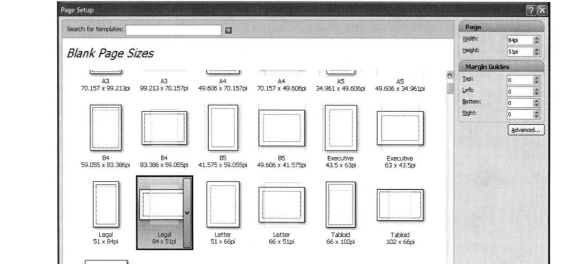

Exhibit 1-2: The Page Setup dialog box

Brochure layout

Brochures typically are printed on a standard-size page and then folded. The fold you use may depend on the kind of information you want to present in the brochure. One common fold is called an *accordion fold*, shown in Exhibit 1-3. With an accordion fold, the layout consists of three or four columns on each side of the page. In Exhibit 1-3, the rightmost column becomes the cover of the brochure when it's folded, and the leftmost column becomes the back of the brochure, which, in this case, is used for the mailing address.

Exhibit 1-3: An example of a brochure with an accordion fold

A-2:   Setting up a brochure

Here's how	Here's why
1 Change the measurement units to picas	(Choose Tools, Options. From the Measurement units list, select picas.) You'll start a brochure by customizing the page size, margin guide, and column guide settings.
2 In the Format Publication pane, click **Change Page Size**	(To open the Page Setup dialog box.) You'll create a two-sided brochure with four columns. When printed, it will use an accordion fold.
Select **Legal (Landscape)**	
Under Margin Guides, set the Top, Left, Bottom, and Right guides to **0**	On the right side of the dialog box.
Click **OK**	To create the publication.
3 Save the publication as **My brochure**	In the current unit folder.
4 Choose **Arrange, Layout Guides...**	To open the Layout Guides dialog box.
5 Activate the Grid Guides tab	
Specify **4 columns**	In the Columns box, change the value to 4.
Set the spacing to **1 pica**	In the Spacing box, change the value to 1pi.
Click **OK**	To close the dialog box.
6 Choose **Insert**, **Page**	To open the Insert Page dialog box.
Click **OK**	A single blank page is inserted after the current page.
7 Save the publication	

Business information

Explanation

A long publication might contain many references to you, your job title, your business address or contact information, or your organization's slogan or logo. Rather than typing or inserting this information every time, you can create a *business information set*, which stores information about you and your organization. If you use a template that includes fields for this information, Publisher will insert it automatically. You can also insert the information yourself. If you change the information in a business set, Publisher will update it in the publication automatically.

To create a business information set:

1 Choose Edit, Business Information.

- If you haven't yet created a business information set, the Create New Business Information Set dialog box opens, as shown in Exhibit 1-4.
- If you've already created a business information set, the Business Information dialog box opens. Click New to create a new set or click Edit to edit an existing set.

2 Enter the appropriate information in the boxes.

3 To add a logo, click Add Logo.

4 In the Business Information set name box, enter an appropriate name.

5 Click Save.

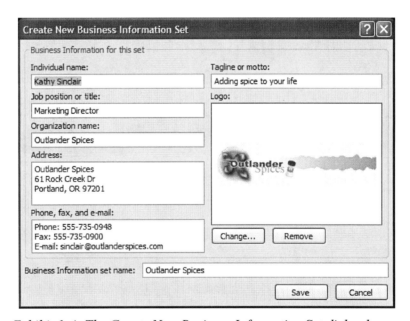

Exhibit 1-4: The Create New Business Information Set dialog box

Do it!   **A-3:   Creating a business information set**

Here's how	Here's why
1 Choose **Edit**, **Business Information...**	To open the Create New Business Information Set dialog box.
2 In the Individual name box, enter your name	
3 Edit the other boxes as indicated in Exhibit 1-4	
4 Click **Add Logo**	The Insert Picture dialog box opens.
Insert **OS logo.tif**	From the current unit folder.
5 Click **Save**	To view the information set in the Business Information dialog box.
Click **Close**	To close the dialog box.

Adding business information

Explanation

After you've created a business information set, you can add relevant business information by using the Business Information pane. The items that you can add have a blue, dotted underline.

- To add an item to an existing text box, place the insertion point, and then double-click the item.
- To add an item in a new text box, first deselect the layout. Then double-click an item in the Business Information pane to create a new text box containing that item.
- You also can drag the item from the Business Information pane onto the layout to create a new text box.

You can include multiple items in a single text box, or you can create different text boxes for each. After you've inserted an item, you can edit it as you would normal text. The items you've inserted from a business information set appear in the layout with blue, dotted underlining. When you point to the item, a smart tag icon appears, as shown in Exhibit 1-5. Click the icon to see a list of options. For example, you can update the business information set based on the text you've edited in the layout, or you can update the text in the layout from the business information set.

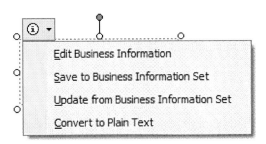

Exhibit 1-5: The smart tag menu for an item in a business information set

Do it!

A-4: Adding business information

Here's how	Here's why
1 From the Other Task Panes list, select **Business Information**	

To activate the Business Information pane. The information you entered in the business information set appears in this pane.

2 Go to page 2	If necessary.
3 Double-click the Address field	To insert the field in the center of the page. A smart tag icon appears above the text box.
4 Move the address text box to the bottom of the third column	
5 Drag the Tagline or motto field to the publication	From the Business Information pane.
Move the Tagline or motto text box to the bottom of the fourth column	
6 Place the logo at the top of the fourth column	
7 Resize and arrange the text boxes as shown	

Outlander Spices
61 Rock Creek Dr
Portland, OR 97201

Adding spice to your life

8 Save and close the publication

Topic B: Custom colors

Explanation

There are several ways that you can create custom colors in Publisher. You can use the default swatches in the Fill Color, Line Color, and Font Color palettes, or you can create swatches of your own in the Colors dialog box. In addition, you can adjust the tint of an existing color swatch to make a lighter version of a color, or you can adjust the shade to make a color darker. You also can create gradients, which are blends of one or more colors.

Color schemes

Publisher uses a default color scheme for new publications. A *color scheme* is the set of default colors that appear in the Fill Color, Line Color, and Font Color palettes, as shown in Exhibit 1-6. The Main color is applied to any elements that you create.

To apply a color scheme to a publication:

1   Open the Format Publication pane.
2   Activate the Color Schemes pane.
3   Click a color scheme to apply it to the current publication.

If you've used any of the default color swatches in the Fill Color, Line Color, or Font Color palettes, those colors will be replaced in your publication by corresponding colors in the new color scheme. For example, the Brown color scheme uses a dark reddish-brown color for the Main color swatch, rather than black. However, any custom colors you've created yourself won't be affected by switching color schemes.

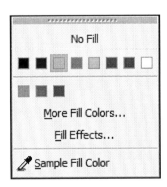

Exhibit 1-6: The colors in the default color scheme (top row)

New color schemes

You can create custom color schemes of your own. To do so, in the Color Schemes pane, click Create new color scheme to open the Create New Color Scheme dialog box, shown in Exhibit 1-7. Under New, select which colors to include in the default set, then edit the Color scheme name box and click Save.

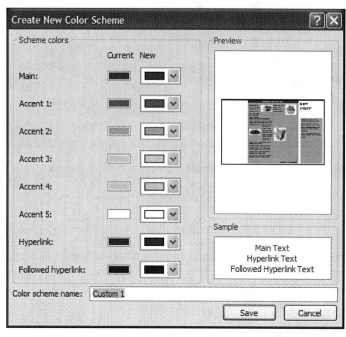

Exhibit 1-7: The Create New Color Scheme dialog box

Do it!

B-1: Changing the color scheme

Here's how	Here's why
1 Open Brochure layout.pub	From the current unit folder.
Save the file as **My Brochure layout**	In the current unit folder.
2 Go to page 2	
Observe the text box in the first and second columns	It's filled with a custom color. When you apply a color scheme, custom colors aren't affected.
Go to page 1	
3 Place the insertion point in either text box that has a fill color	
Show the Fill Color list	On the Formatting toolbar, click the arrow next to the Fill Color button.
Point to the indicated color swatch	
	The text box uses the fill color Accent 2 (Gold).
4 Observe the fill color used in the text box at the top of the page	(The text box containing the text, "A sample from our Pocket Guide to Spices.") The text box uses the Main (Black) fill color.
5 From the Other Task Panes list, select **Color Schemes**	To open the Format Publication pane, with the Color Schemes section active.
From the Apply a color scheme list, select **Brown**	The current color scheme is Bluebird.
Observe the layout	The fill colors for the text boxes have changed, and the text that uses the Main color is now dark brown instead of black.
6 Go to page 2 and observe the fill colors	Two text boxes on this page use a fill color. However, it's a custom color, so it remains unchanged when you change color schemes.
7 Save the publication	

Tint and shade swatches

You can further customize colors by using tints and shades. *Tint* refers to the percentage of white mixed with a particular ink. *Shade* refers to the percentage of black mixed with an ink. For example, a 30% tint of a blue color would use three parts blue and seven parts white—a 0% tint would be pure white. Likewise, a 30% shade would use three parts blue and seven parts black—a 0% shade would be pure black.

To create a tint or shade swatch, select Fill Effects from the Fill Color list. The Fill Effects dialog box opens, as shown in Exhibit 1-8. Activate the Tint tab and select a tint or shade option. If the color you want does not appear in the Fill Effects dialog box, you can select it from the Base color list (or create a new color).

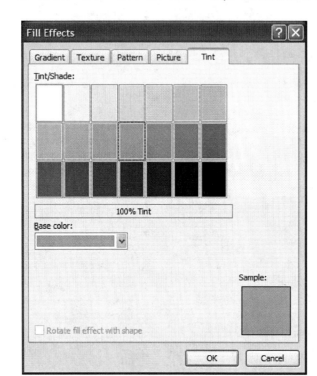

Exhibit 1-8: The Fill Effects dialog box, with the 100% Tint swatch selected

Do it! **B-2: Creating tint swatches**

Here's how	Here's why
1 Go to page 1	
2 Select the text box containing the spice images	You'll make the fill color a tint of the current color.
3 From the Fill Color list, select **Fill Effects...**	To open the Fill Effects dialog box.
Activate the **Tint** tab	
Select the indicated tint	The 30% Tint.
Click **OK**	
4 Observe the Fill Color list	The tint swatch appears in the list. It also appears in the Line Color and Font Color lists.
5 Save the publication	

Gradients

Explanation

A *gradient* is a blend of one or more colors, in which the colors appear along a spectrum with the colors blending where they meet. (If you select one color for a gradient, you can choose to blend it with a darker or lighter version of the same color.) To fill objects with a gradient, use the Gradient tab in the Fill Effects dialog box. You can also control the colors in the gradient, the transparency of the colors, and the shading style of the gradient.

To create a gradient swatch with two colors:

1 Select an object that you want to fill with a gradient.

2 From the Fill Color list, select Fill Effects. The Fill Effects dialog box opens with the Gradient tab active, as shown in Exhibit 1-9.

3 Select Two colors.

4 From the Color 1 list, select the first color to blend.

5 From the Color 2 list, select the second color to blend.

6 If desired, set the transparency of one or both of the colors by dragging the From and To sliders or editing the values in the boxes under Transparency.

7 If desired, select a different option under shading style. The Variants section shows a preview of the style, plus three other options for the style. (The top-left box shows the default variant for that style.)

8 If desired, select a variant of the style by clicking a box under Variants.

9 If you want the gradient to rotate when you rotate the shape it fills, verify that Rotate fill effect with shape is checked.

10 Click OK.

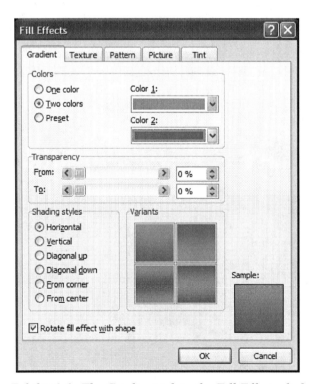

Exhibit 1-9: The Gradient tab in the Fill Effects dialog box

Do it!

B-3:   Creating a gradient

Here's how	Here's why
1 Select the brown text box in the fourth column	You'll apply a gradient fill to this text box.
2 Open the Fill Effects dialog box	From the Fill Color list, select Fill Effects.
Activate the **Gradient** tab	If necessary.
3 Under Colors, select **Two colors**	You'll blend two colors.
4 From the Color 1 list, select the indicated color	The light green color.
From the Color 2 list, select the indicated color	The dark green color.
5 Under Transparency, edit the From box to read **50**	(Publisher will automatically append the % sign.) Later, you'll add a picture that's stacked behind the text box—you want part of it to show through.
6 Under Shading styles, verify that Horizontal is selected	
Observe the Sample box	Color 1, on the top, blends horizontally into Color 2, on the bottom.
7 Click **OK**	To close the dialog box and apply the gradient fill to the text box.
8 Save and close the publication	

Tell students that the sample swatch won't change when they adjust the gradient.

More Colors...
Fill Effects...

Topic C: The Content Library

Explanation

Keeping track of commonly used items can help you work with your publications more effectively. For example, you might have a company logo or some pictures that you need to use in multiple publications. The *Content Library* is a task pane that you can use to store items such as text, graphics, or shapes.

Adding items to the Content Library

Items in the Content Library are not dependent on any particular publication, so you can apply them in any publication you're working on. Likewise, you can add items from any publication. To add items to the Content Library:

1 Open the Content Library pane, shown in Exhibit 1-10.

2 Select an item on the layout that you want to add.

3 In the Content Library pane, click Add selected items to Content Library. The Add Item to Content Library dialog box opens, as shown in Exhibit 1-11.

4 If desired, edit the Title box to name the item.

5 If desired, check one or more options in the Categories list to associate the item or items with a category.

6 Click OK.

You can also add multiple items from a layout as a group to the Content Library. To do so, select all of the items you want to add, and then click Add selected items to Content Library. Publisher remembers their location relative to one another on the layout. You can add the items as a group to a layout and then arrange or delete them individually.

In the Add Item to Content Library dialog box, you can add your own categories to the Categories list. To do so, click Edit Category List to open the Edit Category List dialog box. From there, you can add, delete, rename, or rearrange categories.

Exhibit 1-10: The Content Library pane

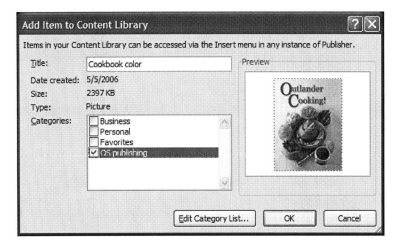

Exhibit 1-11: The Add Item to Content Library dialog box

C-1: Adding an item to the Content Library

Here's how	Here's why
1 Open Flyer.pub	(From the current unit folder.) You'll add the graphics from this publication to the Content Library.
Save the publication as **My Flyer**	
2 From the Other Task Panes list, select **Content Library**	To open the Content Library pane, which is currently empty.
3 Select the cookbook graphic	In the layout.
In the Content Library pane, click **Add selected items to Content Library**	(The link is at the bottom of the pane.) To open the Add Item to Content Library dialog box.
4 Edit the Title box to read **Cookbook color**	
5 Click **Edit Category List**	To open the Edit Category List dialog box.
Click **Add**	
Type **OS publishing**	
Click **OK**	To add the category to the Categories list.
6 In the Categories list, check **OS publishing**	To associate the image you're adding with that category.
Click **OK**	

Content Library

Sort by: Most Recently Used ▾

Cookboo...
Created:1...
Last Used...
Type:Picture
Size:2397 KB

	To close the dialog box. The item now appears in the Content Library.

| 7 Add the gray pepper graphic to the Content Library in the OS publishing category | Select the image; then, in the Content Library pane, click Add selected items to Content Library. In the Add Item to Content Library dialog box, in the Categories list, check OS publishing, and click OK. |
| 8 Save and close the publication | |

Placing Content Library items

Explanation

To place Content Library items in a publication, drag them from the Content Library pane to the publication window. If there are a large number of objects in the Content Library, you can quickly locate the item you want by selecting an option from the Category and/or Type lists in the Content Library pane.

Do it!

C-2: Inserting an item from the Content Library

Here's how	Here's why
1 Open My Brochure layout.pub	
2 Open the Content Library pane	(From the Other Task Panes list, select Content Library.) The items that you added from the Flyer publication appear in the Content Library.
3 Drag the cookbook image from the Content Library onto page 1	
Place and size the image as shown	
4 Go to page 2	
5 Drag the pepper image to page 2	Drag it from the Content Library onto the page.
6 Place and resize the image so that it fits the width of the first two columns, as shown	
	You'll send the image to the back of the stacking order, to make the image a "watermark" over which the text can be read.

Tell students to drag a corner handle to resize the image.

7	Choose **Arrange**, **Order**, **Send to Back**	To move the graphic to the back of the stacking order. The text box is filled with a color that hides the image. You'll adjust the transparency of the fill color so that the pepper image appears as a watermark.
8	Select the green text box	
9	Open the Format Text Box dialog box	Choose Format, Text Box.
	Under Fill, edit the Transparency box to read **30**	(On the Colors and Lines tab.) Publisher will automatically append the % sign.
	Click **OK**	
10	Save the publication	

Topic D: The Graphics Manager pane

Explanation

You can use the Graphics Manager pane to manage the pictures in your publication. It provides an easy way to replace a picture in your publication with another picture and to link or embed a picture. The Graphics Manager pane also displays detailed information about a picture, such as its size or file type.

Picture details

The Graphics Manager pane lists all the pictures in a publication, and the details about each picture. To view a picture's details, point to the picture, and then click the arrow and select Details to open the Details dialog box, shown in Exhibit 1-13.

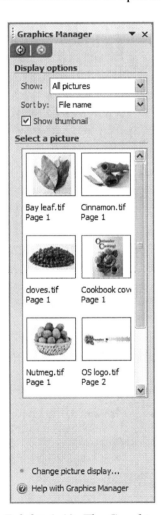

Exhibit 1-12: The Graphics Manager pane

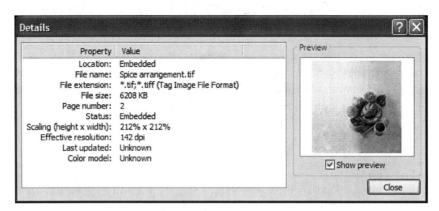

Exhibit 1-13: The Details dialog box

Linked and embedded pictures

You also can use the Graphics Manager pane to link an embedded picture or embed a linked picture. A *linked picture* is saved separately from the publication. A low-resolution preview of the picture appears in the publication, but it isn't included with the publication. Therefore, if you send the publication to a printing press, for example, you'll have to manually include the image as well.

It can be a good idea to link pictures if they have large file sizes, because this can increase the file size of your publication significantly, making it more difficult to send via e-mail or upload and download it on the Internet. If you want to ensure that the picture is included with the publication, you can *embed* the picture. Embedding a picture places the full-resolution image directly in the layout, so you don't need the originals when sending the publication to a printing press.

By default, Publisher embeds pictures. You can tell whether a picture is linked or embedded by looking at the Select a picture list in the Graphics Manager pane (if Show thumbnail is cleared), or by opening the Details dialog box for that picture. To convert an embedded picture to a linked picture:

1 In the Graphics Manager pane, point to an embedded picture and click the arrow to display the menu.
2 Select Save as Linked Picture to open the Save As dialog box.
3 Navigate to the location where you want to save the picture. (It's a good idea to save the picture in the same folder as the publication it belongs to.)
4 If desired, edit the File name box.
5 Click Save.

Selecting underlying items

Sometimes you might need to select an item that's positioned underneath another item and is therefore difficult or impossible to select directly. If the underlying item is a picture, it will appear in the Graphics Manager pane. To select it, click the name of the picture in the Select a picture list (in the Graphics Manager pane).

Do it!

D-1:   Linking a picture

Here's how	Here's why
1 Open the Graphics Manager pane	From the Other Task Panes list, select Graphics Manager.
Observe the Select a picture list	Every picture in the current publication is listed. By default, any pictures that you insert are embedded, but this can greatly increase the file size.
2 Check **Show thumbnail**	To view thumbnails of the pictures.
3 In the Select a picture list, select **Spice arrangement**	(Scroll down.) The image is selected on the page.
4 Next to the picture's thumbnail, click the arrow	To show the list of options.
Select **Details...**	To open the Details dialog box.
5 Observe the picture details	To confirm that it's currently embedded, and to note its file size (6208 KB, or slightly more than 6 MB). You'll make this a linked picture in order to reduce the file size of the publication.
Click **Close**	
6 Click the arrow again, and select **Save as Linked picture...**	To open the Save As dialog box.
Navigate to the current unit folder, and click **Save**	
7 In the Graphics Manager pane, clear **Show thumbnail**	To show the list of pictures, indicating which are linked and which are embedded.
Observe the selected item	OS logo.tif (Page 2) Embedded (1256 KB) Spice arrangement.png (Page Linked (3171 KB) Watermark pepper.tif (Page 2) Embedded (1421 KB)
	To verify that the picture is now linked.
8 Save the publication	

If there's time, have students note the size of the publication in Windows Explorer both before and after linking the picture.

Point out that this information also is shown in the Select a picture list.

Replacing a picture

Explanation

You can use the Graphics Manager pane to quickly replace a picture:

1 Open the Graphics Manager pane.
2 Point to the picture to be replaced and click the arrow to display the menu.
3 Choose Replace this Picture to open the Insert Picture dialog box.
4 Select the picture you want to insert.
5 Click Insert to replace the picture.

Do it!

D-2: Replacing a picture

Here's how	Here's why
1 Go to page 1	You'll replace the cookbook picture with another image.
2 Show the options for the Cookbook cover	In the Graphics Manager pane, point to the image name, and then click the arrow.
Select **Replace this Picture...**	To open the Insert Picture dialog box.
3 Select **Cookbook reflection.tif**	From the current unit folder.
Click **Insert**	To replace the picture.
4 Resize the picture as shown	

Notice that the text in the text box it overlaps automatically wraps to accommodate the image.

5 Send the picture to the back of the stacking order	(Choose Arrange, Order, Send to Back.) So that it doesn't cause the text to wrap.
6 Save and close the publication	

Unit summary: Basic design options

Topic A   In this topic, you explored **publication templates** and set up a **brochure**. Then, you created a **business information set** and added information to it.

Topic B   In this topic, you learned how to change a publication's **color scheme**. You also used the Fill Effects dialog box to create **tint swatches** and **gradients**.

Topic C   In this topic, you learned how to add an item to the **Content Library** and then insert objects from the Content Library into a layout.

Topic D   In this topic, you learned how to use the **Graphics Manager** to **link an embedded picture** and to **replace a picture** with another picture.

Independent practice activity

In this activity, you'll insert business information in a publication. Then you'll create a tint swatch, and use the Content Library and the Graphics Manager.

1 Open Practice layout.pub (from the current unit folder), and save it as **My Practice layout**.

2 Go to page 6. (There's a horizontal guide indicating the middle of the page, where the newsletter will be folded for mailing. Below the guide, in the first column, there's a text box.)

3 From the Business Information pane, insert the Address information into the text box. (*Hint*: First, place the insertion point in the text box.)

4 Go to page 1. The newsletter uses a custom color for some elements, such as headings and horizontal rules. Create a swatch that uses a 60% shade of the color.

5 In the first column, there's a text box that lists the contents of the newsletter. Create a gradient to fill the text box, using two colors: blending horizontally from the custom green color to the shade you created.

6 Go to page 4, and add the pictures on this page to the Content Library.

7 On page 2, use the Graphics Manager to replace the picture of the cookbooks with the Cookbook reflection picture (in the current unit folder).

8 Save and close the publication.

Review questions

1 Which dialog box would you use to change only a publication's page size?

A Layout Guides

B Page Setup

C Change Template

D Print Setup

2 Which of the following is *not* a method for adding business information from the Business Information pane?

A Place the insertion point, then double-click the item in the pane.

B Deselect all layout elements, then double-click the item in the pane.

C Drag the item from the task pane onto the layout.

D Begin typing the information, and Publisher will automatically finish it.

3 You've set the fill color for a text box using a custom color, but now you want to change the color scheme for the publication. What do you have to do to ensure that the custom color remains unaffected?

Nothing. Changing the color scheme doesn't affect items that use a custom color.

4 Explain the difference between tint and shade.

Tint refers to the percentage of white mixed with a particular ink. Shade refers to the percentage of black mixed with an ink.

5 If you select two items on a layout and add them to the Content Library, what happens?

A They each are added separately.

B Publisher adds only the first item you selected.

C Publisher remembers their position relative to one another.

D An error message appears because you can only add one item at a time to the Content Library.

6 How can you organize items in the Content Library so that you can locate them quickly?

In the Add Item to Content Library dialog box, you can add your own categories to the Categories list or select from existing ones. In the Content Library pane, you can quickly locate categorized items by selecting an option from the Category and/or Type lists.

7 What's the difference between a linked picture and an embedded picture?

A linked picture is saved separately from the publication—a low-resolution preview of the picture appears in the publication, but it isn't included with the publication. Embedding the picture places the full-resolution picture directly in the layout.

8 You want to select a picture that's completely covered by a text box. How can you do this?

In the Graphics Manager pane, click the name or thumbnail of the picture you want to select; it will be selected in the layout.

U n i t   2

Typography

Unit time: 90 minutes

Complete this unit, and you'll know how to:

A Work with styles and change the font scheme.

B Insert WordArt, create a type mask by modifying a WordArt object, and modify text wrap based on image contours.

C Snap text to a baseline guide and distribute text horizontally.

D Insert symbols and special characters.

Topic A: Styles and font schemes

Explanation

Styles are formatting options that define the appearance of recurring text components, such as headings or body text. By using a style, you can apply several formatting options in one step. For example, if you want all section headings in a publication to display with the Arial font face in bold at 16 points, you can create and name a style with these properties, and then apply that style to each section heading, rather than repeating each individual formatting option every time. Styles can help you maintain formatting consistency within and among publications.

The Styles pane

Publisher provides several predefined styles. For example, you can apply the Heading 1 style to format selected text as a heading. By default, when you create a new document, Publisher applies the Normal style to the entire document.

Examining a style

You can preview a style's formatting in the Styles pane, as shown in Exhibit 2-1. You also can point to a style's name, and a ScreenTip will show the formatting information for that style. To view all formatting for a particular style, point to the style name and click the down arrow. Then, select Modify to open the Modify Style dialog box, shown in Exhibit 2-2. Under Click to change, click to view formatting for Font, Character spacing, etc.

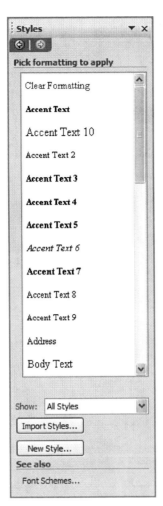

Exhibit 2-1: The Styles pane

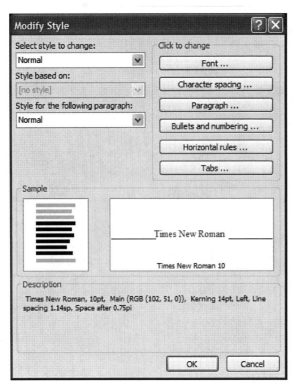

Exhibit 2-2: The Modify Style dialog box

Do it!

A-1: Examining a style

Here's how	Here's why
1 Open Brochure typography.pub	From the current unit folder.
Save it as **My Brochure typography**	In the current unit folder.
2 Place the insertion point in any text box	
3 Open the Styles pane	
Scroll through the predefined styles in the list	Publisher includes several predefined styles. Currently, all the text in this publication is in the Normal style, which is the default style.
4 Point to the Normal style, and click the arrow	To display a menu.
Select **Modify...**	To open the Modify Style dialog box.
5 Read the information in the Description box	To verify the font, font size, font color, and other attributes of this style.
6 Click **Cancel**	To close the dialog box.

Creating styles

Explanation

If you plan to repeatedly use the same combinations of text formatting options, you can create a new style. If you've already formatted some text in your layout using a combination of options that you want to apply to other text, you can base a new style on that formatting.

To create a new style:

1   Decide if you want to create a style from scratch or based on existing formatting:

   • To create a new style from scratch, first deselect any text boxes by clicking the scratch area or a blank area of the layout.

   • To base a new style on existing formatting, first select the text on which you want to base the new style.

2   In the Styles pane, click New Style to open the New Style dialog box, which is identical to the Modify Style dialog box, shown in Exhibit 2-2.

3   Enter a name for the new style.

4   By default, a new style is based on the Normal style. To base the style on a different style, select it from the Style based on list.

5   Under Click to change, adjust the desired formatting by clicking Font, Character Spacing, etc., to open the respective dialog boxes.

6   After you've finished applying the desired formatting, click OK to create the style.

Styles for following paragraphs

When you create a style, you can specify that a paragraph following that style will automatically use a particular style. For example, if your publication has a particular type of heading that you've created a style for, and you want the text after each of these headings to have a particular style, you can select a style from the Style for following paragraph list, in the New Style or Modify Style dialog box.

Do it!

A-2:   Creating a style

Here's how	Here's why
1 Click the scratch area	To ensure that no text is selected.
2 In the Styles pane, click **New Style**	To open the New Style dialog box.
3 In the Enter new style name box, enter **Spice guide**	You'll use this style for the text in the middle columns of page 1, which is an example from another Outlander Spices publication. If you were to substitute different text from that publication, you could apply the style to that text to retain the same formatting.
4 Click **Font**	To open the Font dialog box.
From the Size list, select **16**	
Click **OK**	To close the dialog box.
5 Click **Paragraph**	To open the Paragraph dialog box.
Under Line spacing, edit the Between lines box to read **1.5sp**	
Edit the After paragraphs box to read **12pt**	
Click **OK**	To close the Paragraph dialog box.
6 Click **OK**	To close the New Style dialog box. You'll apply the new style shortly.
7 Save the publication	

Remind students that they can use the arrows or enter values manually.

Basing styles on existing styles

Explanation

When you create a new style, you can choose to base it on an existing style. The new style will inherit the formatting options from the style you choose to base it on, and any additional formatting options you select will either replace or be added to the inherited options. For example, say you create a new style for a section heading named "Appendix Heading." You want the Appendix Heading style to have all the same formatting options as the style Heading 1, but you also want the text to be green. Rather than manually repeating the formatting of Heading 1, you can base the new style on it and then select the font color for the new style.

To base a new style on an existing style:

1 In the Styles pane, click New Style.

2 Enter a name for the new style.

3 From the Style based on list, select an existing style on which to base the new style.

4 Select any other formatting options you want to apply to the new style. Any formatting options you select will override the formatting from the "based on" style.

5 Click OK.

Do it!   **A-3:   Basing a style on an existing style**

Here's how	Here's why
1 Open the New Style dialog box	In the Styles pane, click New Style.
2 Name the new style **Cover text**	(Enter the name in the Enter new style name box.) You'll use all the same settings as the Spice guide style, except line spacing.
3 From the Style based on list, select **Spice guide**	
4 Set the line spacing for the style to **2sp**, and click **OK**	Click Paragraph, then edit the Between lines box.
Observe the Description box	Description Spice guide + Line spacing 2sp
	The style uses the settings for the spice guide style, plus the line spacing you specified.
5 Click **OK**	To close the New Style dialog box.
6 Create a new style based on the Spice guide style	
Name the style "Inside text"	
Set the line spacing for the new style to **1.25sp**	
7 Save the publication	

Applying styles

Explanation

You can apply a style to selected text by opening the Styles pane and selecting the desired style from the list. But it might be inconvenient to open the Styles pane every time you want to apply a style. You also can apply styles to selected text by selecting the desired style from the Style list on the Formatting toolbar.

Do it!

A-4: Applying a style

Here's how	Here's why
1 On page 1, click anywhere inside the text	
Press CTRL + A	To select all the text in the two columns.
2 In the Styles pane, select the style **Spice guide**	(Scroll down to access the style.) The selected text is formatted with the new style properties.
3 Select the text shown	

Apply the style "Cover text" to the selection	Scroll up in the list.
4 On page 2, select all the text in the large green text box	
Apply the style "Inside text" to the selection	
5 Select the text in the text box at the top of the third column	
Apply the "Inside text" style to the selection	The text overflows the text box. You'll fix this in the next activity by overriding the style.

Overriding styles

Explanation

As you work in a publication, you might want to change the formatting of text after you've applied a style to it. For example, after applying the Heading 1 style, you might decide to increase the heading font to 20pt. You can do this by selecting the text and applying the desired formatting. This action overrides the formatting contained in that instance of the style, and does not affect the style itself.

Modifying styles

To modify a style, point to the style name in the Styles pane, then click the down arrow and select Modify. When you modify a style this way, the style itself is altered, so the changes will apply to all text that uses the style.

Deleting styles

You can also delete a style by using the Styles pane. To do so, point to the name of the style that you want to delete, click the down-arrow to the right of the style name, and choose Delete. You'll be prompted to confirm the deletion. When you delete a style, text that has been formatted with that style will revert to the Normal style.

Do it!

A-5:   Overriding and modifying a style

Here's how	Here's why
1 On page 2, observe the text in the first and second columns	The font originally was white. Applying the new style changed it to the default color.
Make the text white again	Select the text. Then, from the Font Color list, select Accent 5 (White). The style now has all the style properties in the "Inside text" style, plus the white font color.
2 Select the text box at the top of the third column	The style's spacing causes the text to overflow the text box. You'll modify the style.
3 In the Styles pane, point to the Inside text style	
Click the arrow and select **Modify...**	To open the Modify Style dialog box.
Change the line spacing for this style to 3pt after each paragraph	Click Paragraph, then edit the After paragraphs box.
4 Verify the results	The text now fits inside the text box. The text has all the style properties of the "Inside text" style, except the after paragraph line spacing.
5 Save the publication	

Font schemes

Explanation

Publisher uses a default font scheme for new publications. A *font scheme* is a set of styles that includes a heading and a body font. Changing the font scheme affects all the text in a publication by default. However, you can choose which text attributes will be affected by a font scheme by using the Font Scheme Options dialog box.

To change the font scheme for a publication, open the Font Schemes pane, shown in Exhibit 2-3. Then click a font scheme to apply it to the current publication.

When you apply a new font scheme, the Font Scheme Options dialog box determines which text attributes will be affected. To open this dialog box from the Font Schemes pane, click Font scheme options. You'll see three options:

- Update custom text styles
- Override applied text formatting
- Adjust font sizes

Clear any of these options that you want Publisher to skip when applying the new font scheme.

Exhibit 2-3: Font schemes

New font schemes

You can create your own font schemes. In the Font Schemes pane, click Create new font scheme to open the Create New Font Scheme dialog box, shown in Exhibit 2-4. Select fonts for the headings and body text from the Heading font and Body font lists; then edit the Font scheme name box and click Save.

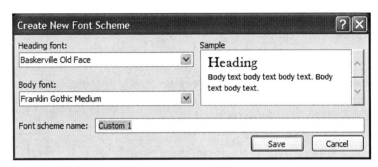

Exhibit 2-4: The Create New Font Scheme dialog box

Do it!

A-6:   Changing the font scheme

Here's how	Here's why
1 Open the Font Schemes pane	The default font scheme is Versatile, which uses Times New Roman for both the heading and the body font.
2 From the Apply a font scheme list, select **Virtual**	(Scroll to the bottom of the list.) To change the heading and body fonts to Trebuchet MS. Throughout the publication, only the font face has changed; all other styles remain the same.
3 Save the publication	

Topic B: Graphics in typography

Explanation

You can use WordArt to create dramatic text effects that regular styles can't achieve. For example, using WordArt, you can create headline text that follows a curve and has a drop shadow.

WordArt

WordArt appears in a publication as a graphic, so you can't edit it directly. You can choose from 30 different WordArt styles, and you can customize each style by editing the text, font, font size, and bold or italic formatting. You can also format a WordArt object's fill and line attributes and its shape.

To insert a WordArt object:

1   On the Objects toolbar, click the Insert WordArt button to open the WordArt Gallery dialog box, shown in Exhibit 2-5.
2   Select a WordArt style to use. (You can change the style later.)
3   Click OK to open the Edit WordArt Text dialog box.
4   If desired, select a font and a font size.
5   If desired, select bold and/or italic formatting.
6   Edit the Text box.
7   Click OK to create the WordArt object.

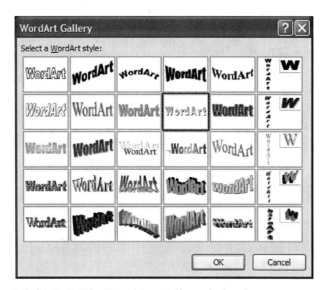

Exhibit 2-5: The WordArt Gallery dialog box

If you want to create a WordArt object from existing text, first select that text, and then begin creating the WordArt object. In the Edit WordArt Text dialog box, the text that you selected will appear.

After you've created a WordArt object, the WordArt toolbar appears, as shown in Exhibit 2-6. Using the WordArt toolbar, you can edit the text, style, formatting, and shape of a WordArt object.

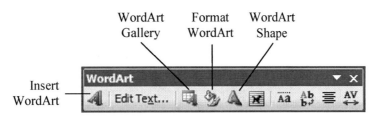

Exhibit 2-6: The WordArt toolbar

B-1: Inserting WordArt

Here's how	Here's why
1 Go to page 2	If necessary.
2 On the Objects toolbar, click [A]	(The Insert WordArt button.) To open the WordArt Gallery dialog box. You'll replace the existing heading with a WordArt object.
Select the indicated WordArt style	
	The fourth option in the second row.
Click **OK**	The Edit WordArt Text dialog box opens.
3 From the Font list, select **Trebuchet MS**	
4 Click **B**	To format the WordArt object in bold.
5 Edit the Text box to read **Quality spices since 1989!**	
Click **OK**	To close the dialog box and create the WordArt object. The WordArt toolbar appears.
6 On the WordArt toolbar, click [✏]	(The Format WordArt button.) To open the Format WordArt dialog box, with the Colors and Lines tab active.
From the Color list, select the dark brown color named Main	
Click **OK**	To close the dialog box.
7 On the WordArt toolbar, click [A]	(The WordArt Shape button.) To display the gallery of WordArt shapes.
From the WordArt Shape gallery, select the indicated shape	

8 Delete the heading at the top of the first and second columns

Tell students to leave the WordArt toolbar open.

9 Drag the WordArt up to replace the heading, as shown

10 Save the publication

Type masks

Explanation

A popular design technique is to use an image as a background for text. This is known as a *type mask*, wherein the image appears only within the characters of the text, as illustrated in Exhibit 2-7. In Publisher, you can achieve this effect by filling a WordArt object with a picture.

To create a type mask:

1 Select a WordArt object.

2 On the WordArt toolbar, click the Format WordArt button to open the Format WordArt dialog box with the Colors and Lines tab active.

3 Under Fill, from the Color list, select Fill Effects to open the Fill Effects dialog box.

4 Activate the Picture tab, which is shown in Exhibit 2-8.

5 Click Select Picture to open the Select Picture dialog box.

6 Select the desired picture, then click Insert.

7 Click OK to close the Fill Effects dialog box.

8 Click OK.

Exhibit 2-7: An example of a type mask

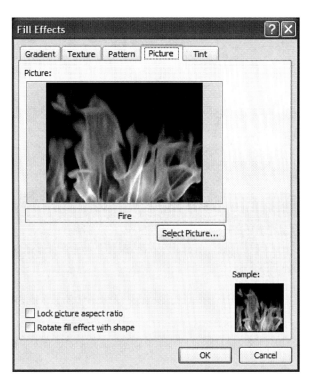

Exhibit 2-8: The Picture tab in the Fill Effects dialog box

B-2: Creating a type mask with WordArt

Here's how	Here's why
1 Go to page 1	
2 Select the heading "Hot Stuff"	Select all the text in the heading.
3 Open the WordArt Gallery dialog box	On the Objects toolbar, click the Insert WordArt button.
Select the indicated WordArt style	
	The same style you applied before.
Click **OK**	To open the Edit WordArt Text dialog box. The selected text appears in the Text box.
4 Make the text bold	Click the bold button. You'll use the default font, which is Arial Black.
Click **OK**	The WordArt object appears in the middle of the page. Notice that basing the WordArt object on existing text does not delete that text.
5 On the WordArt toolbar, click ▤	(The WordArt Alignment button.) To display a list of options.
Select **Left Align**	
6 On the WordArt toolbar, click [Aa]	(The WordArt Same Letter Heights button.) To make all the characters in the WordArt object the same height.
7 Delete the original "HOT STUFF" heading	(Select and delete the text box.) You'll replace it with the new WordArt object.
Drag the WordArt object into the empty space	To create a new heading for the column.

⚠ Make sure that students select all the text.

Point out that the text on which the WordArt is based was not deleted.

8 Drag the resize handles to resize the WordArt object as shown

9 Click the Format WordArt button

(On the WordArt toolbar.) To open the Format WordArt dialog box.

Under Fill, from the Color list, select **Fill Effects**

To open the Fill Effects dialog box.

10 Activate the **Picture** tab

Click **Select Picture**

To open the Select Picture dialog box.

Select **Fire.jpg**

From the current unit folder.

Click **Insert**

The picture appears in the Fill Effects dialog box.

Click **OK**

To close the Fill Effects dialog box.

11 Click **OK**

The WordArt object is now filled with the selected picture, which creates the type mask effect.

Close the WordArt toolbar

12 Save the publication

Contour-based text wraps

Explanation

Previously, you learned how to apply text wraps to picture frames, so that text flows around the outside of the frame. At times, you might want the text to flow around a specific portion of a graphic. You can achieve this by applying a text wrap to a graphic based on image contours.

To apply a path-based text wrap:

1   Select the graphic.
2   Open the Format Picture dialog box.
3   Activate the Layout tab.
4   Under Wrapping Style, select Through.
5   Click OK.

Sometimes, wrapping text around an image's contours might produce undesirable effects, such as one word appearing at the bottom-left edge of an image and the rest of the text flowing to the right. If this happens, open the Format Picture dialog box and activate the Layout tab. Under Wrap text, select an option to force the text to wrap to the left, right, or in the largest space available.

Do it!

B-3:   Wrapping text based on image contours

Here's how	Here's why
1 In the second column, select the cinnamon image	You'll adjust the text wrap so that the text wraps based in the image's contours.
2 Open the Format Picture dialog box	Choose Format, Picture.
Activate the **Layout** tab	
Under Wrapping Style, select **Through**	
Click **OK**	To close the dialog box. The text now flows more closely underneath the image.
3 Apply the same wrap setting to the remaining three spice images	Select an image. In the Format Picture dialog box, activate the Layout tab. Under Wrapping Style, select Through.
4 Save the publication	

Tell students they can undo the last change to see how the text wrapped previously, then click Redo to apply the formatting again.

Tell students to leave the publication open.

Topic C: Precise spacing control

Explanation

Setting a specific spacing value for text often does not guarantee that everything will align perfectly in a layout. In addition to equal spacing between lines, you'll usually want the text to align horizontally from column to column. You can use baseline guides to ensure that text in adjacent columns is aligned properly, and you can distribute text horizontally if you want a line of text to fill a particular space, even if there are too few characters to fill the space automatically.

Baseline guides

Baseline guides are a set of non-printing lines that run along the width of a publication page to align columns of text. For example, if there are two columns on a page, the lines of text in one column should match up with the adjacent lines of text in the other column. In Exhibit 2-9, you can see that often this isn't the case, either because the columns are positioned differently on the page or because one column contains some text with different spacing.

Exhibit 2-9: Two adjacent columns with misaligned text

Baseline guides are not visible by default. To display them, choose View, Baseline Guides. This is a good way to verify that your columns of text are aligned correctly.

To align misaligned text to baseline guides:

1 First, determine the desired spacing of the text. For example, if the paragraphs of two adjacent text boxes use 15pt spacing, you might want to set the baseline guides 15pt apart.

2 Choose View, Baseline Guides to display the baseline guides.

3 Choose Arrange, Layout Guides to open the Layout Guides dialog box, and activate the Baseline Guides tab, shown in Exhibit 2-10.

4 Edit the Spacing box to set the spacing between baseline guides.

5 If desired, edit the Offset box to adjust the space between the top margin of the page and the first baseline guide.

6 Close the dialog box.

7 Select the text that you want to align to the baseline guides, or, if you want to align text that uses a particular style, then open the Modify Style dialog box for the desired style.

8 In the Paragraph dialog box, check Align text to baseline guides.

9 Close the dialog box.

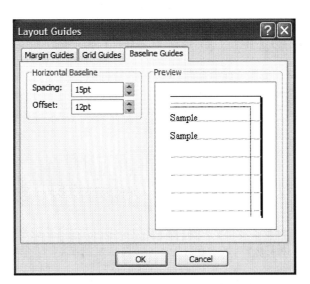

Exhibit 2-10: The Baseline Guides tab in the Layout Guides dialog box

C-1: Snapping text to a baseline guide

Here's how	Here's why
1 Open Newsletter.pub	From the current unit folder.
Save it as **My Newsletter**	In the current unit folder.
2 Choose **View**, **Baseline Guides**	To show the baseline guides.
3 Zoom in on the text in the second and third columns	

(image of two columns of text from the "Spices of the Month" article: "Bay leaves come in many varieties. The popular American variety, known as sweet bay and laurel, is a kitchen staple used widely to flavor meats, soups, stews, gravies, and vegetable dishes. The elliptical leaves are green, glossy, and generally grow to about 3 inches in length. / bit of cheesecloth. Add other herbs as the nature of the dish and your whims dictate. Try adding lemon, sage, and tarragon with chicken; rosemary and mint with lamb; green peppercorns, orange, and savory to beef. Old, dried leaves tend to lose their flavor, so be sure to replenish your supply often.")

(The beginning of the "Spices of the Month" article.) The two columns of text don't line up.

4 Place the insertion point in the first paragraph of the article	Under the "Bay Leaves" heading.
Open the Paragraph dialog box	Choose Format, Paragraph.
Observe the line spacing	The Between lines box reads 15pt. You'll space the baseline guides 15 points apart.
Click **Cancel**	To close the dialog box.
5 Choose **Arrange**, **Layout Guides…**	To open the Layout Guides dialog box.
Activate the **Baseline Guides** tab	
Edit the Spacing box to read **15pt**	
Click **OK**	To close the dialog box.
6 Open the Styles pane	The text has a style applied to it. You'll modify the style so that all of the text using that style will snap to the baseline guides.
7 Open the Modify Style dialog box for the Newsletter story style	
8 Click **Paragraph**	To open the Paragraph dialog box.
Check **Align text to baseline guides**	
Click **OK**	To close the dialog box.

TIPS *Tell students they can also press Ctrl+F7.*

9 Click **OK**

> **B**ay leaves come in many varieties. The popular American variety, known as sweet bay and laurel, is a kitchen staple used widely to flavor meats, soups, stews, gravies, and vegetable dishes. The elliptical leaves are green, glossy, and generally grow to about 3 inches in length.
>
> cooking. Dried herbs can be substituted and tied in a bit of cheesecloth. Add other herbs as the nature of the dish and your whims dictate. Try adding lemon, sage, and tarragon with chicken; rosemary and mint with lamb; green peppercorns, orange, and savory to beef. Old, dried leaves tend to lose their flavor,

The text is now aligned across columns.

10 Save and close the publication

Horizontal distribution

Explanation

You might want some text to fill the width of a text box, regardless of the number of characters in a line. For example, you might want a heading to stretch across the top of a page, even if the heading doesn't contain enough characters to fill the space automatically. To distribute text horizontally in a text box:

1 Select the text.

2 Open the Paragraph dialog box.

3 From the Alignment list, select Distribute All Lines.

4 Close the dialog box.

Do it!

C-2: Distributing text horizontally

The previous publication should still be open.

Here's how	Here's why
1 Go to page 2	In the My Brochure typography publication.
2 In the fourth column, select the text "Pocket Guide to SPICES"	You'll format the text so that it stretches to fill the text box.
3 Open the Paragraph dialog box	
From the Alignment list, select **Distribute All Lines**	To distribute the lines to fill the text box.
Click **OK**	To close the dialog box. The text now fills the text box horizontally.
4 Save the publication	

Topic D: Symbols and special characters

Explanation

If your document includes non-English words, references to currency, or copyright notices, you'll probably need to use symbols and characters that aren't available on a standard keyboard. Publisher inserts some symbols automatically; for example, if you type "(c)" Publisher converts the text to the copyright symbol, "©." Others are available in the Symbol dialog box.

Symbols

Symbols are standard characters that you might need from time to time, but are not available on a keyboard. To insert symbols:

1   Place the insertion point where you want to insert the symbol.

2   Choose Insert, Symbol to open the Symbol dialog box, shown in Exhibit 2-11.

3   To view the symbols available for a particular font, select it from the Font list.

4   To see a subset of available symbols (for example, Currency Symbols), select it from the Subset list.

5   Select the symbol that you want to insert.

6   Click Insert to insert the symbol.

7   Click Close.

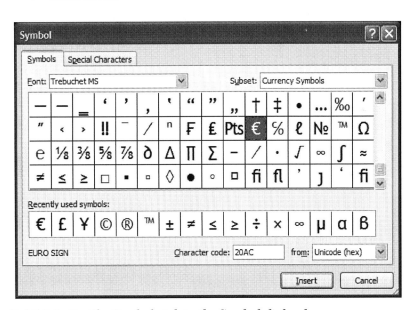

Exhibit 2-11: The Symbols tab in the Symbol dialog box

Do it!   **D-1:   Inserting symbols**

Here's how	Here's why
1 In the third column, delete the word "Euros"	You'll replace it with the Euro symbol.
Delete the extra space after the number 8	If necessary.
2 Place the insertion point before the 8	
3 Choose **Insert, Symbol...**	To open the Symbol dialog box with the Symbols tab active.
4 From the Subset list, select **Currency Symbols**	
Select the indicated symbol	
Click **Insert**	To insert the symbol at the insertion point.
5 Click **Close**	To close the dialog box.
6 Save the publication	

Special characters

Explanation   Special characters include things such as copyright, registered, and trademark symbols, and other characters not available on standard keyboards.

To insert special characters:

1   Place the insertion point where you want to insert the symbol.
2   Choose Insert, Symbol to open the Symbol dialog box.
3   Activate the Special Characters tab.
4   Select the character that you want to insert.
5   Click Insert to insert the character.
6   Click Close.

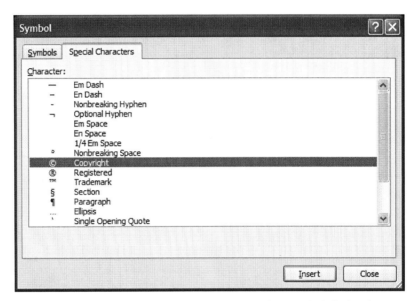

Exhibit 2-12: The Special Characters tab in the Symbol dialog box

Em dashes, en dashes, and hyphens

Em dashes, en dashes, and hyphens look similar but are of different lengths and are used for different purposes. You use a *hyphen* typically to combine compound words; it's the shortest of the three. An *en dash* is longer and is typically used in place of "through," such as in "pages 3–15." An *em dash* is what typically is meant by "dash"—a strong break (such as this one) in the flow of a sentence—and is the longest of the three. When using either an em dash, en dash, or hyphen, you don't need to put spaces on either side.

Do it!

D-2:   Inserting special characters

Here's how	Here's why
1 Go to page 1	
Zoom in on the Copyright statement	At the bottom of page.
2 Place the insertion point after the word "Copyright"	At the bottom of the third column.
Press (SPACEBAR)	
3 Open the Symbol dialog box	Choose Insert, Symbol.
Activate the **Special Characters** tab	
4 From the Character list, select **Copyright**	
Click **Insert**	
Click **Close**	
5 Save and close the publication	

Help students locate the word.

Unit summary: Typography

Topic A   In this topic, you learned how to create and apply **styles**, create styles based on existing styles, and override, modify, and delete styles. You also learned how to create and apply **font schemes**.

Topic B   In this topic, you learned how to use **WordArt** to create text effects that regular styles can't achieve. You also created a **type mask**, and you **wrapped text** around the contours of an image.

Topic C   In this topic, you learned how to snap text to a **baseline guide** to ensure proper text alignment between adjacent columns, and you learned how to **distribute text horizontally**.

Topic D   In this topic, you learned how to insert **symbols** and **special characters**.

Independent practice activity

In this activity, you'll work with styles and a WordArt object, and insert symbols.

1 Open Practice typography.pub (from the current unit folder), and save it as **My Practice typography**.

2 On page 2, give the headline "Outlander Spice Collection!" a dark green color. (*Hint*: Use one of the currently defined colors.)

3 Create a new style named **Headline 1** based on the headline.

4 Apply the Headline 1 style to the headings on pages 2 and 3. The specified font size is too large for the heading "Cooking with Outlander!"

5 Make the heading "Cooking with Outlander!" **15pt**.

6 Modify the Headline 1 style so that the spacing for the horizontal rule is **0pi** from the right margin.

7 On page 5, apply the Headline 1 style to the heading "Note from the President."

8 On page 4, delete the heading "Chicken Stuffed with Spices". Then create a WordArt heading using the style indicated in Exhibit 2-13. Use Trebuchet MS, bold, for the font.

9 Resize and position the WordArt object as shown in Exhibit 2-14.

10 On page 5, view the "Four New Locations" story at 100%.

11 In the second paragraph, replace the "e" in both instances of "cafe" with the symbol "é," as shown in Exhibit 2-15. In addition, replace the second "e" in "entree" with the same symbol, to make it "entrée."

12 Save and close the publication.

WordArt Gallery
Change the WordArt style:
OK
Cancel

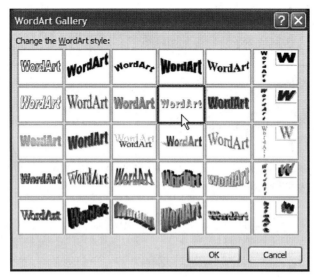

Exhibit 2-13: The WordArt style applied in step 8

Outlander Spices
Chicken Stuffed with Spices

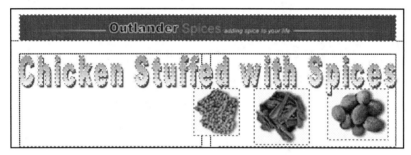

Exhibit 2-14: The WordArt object's appearance after step 9

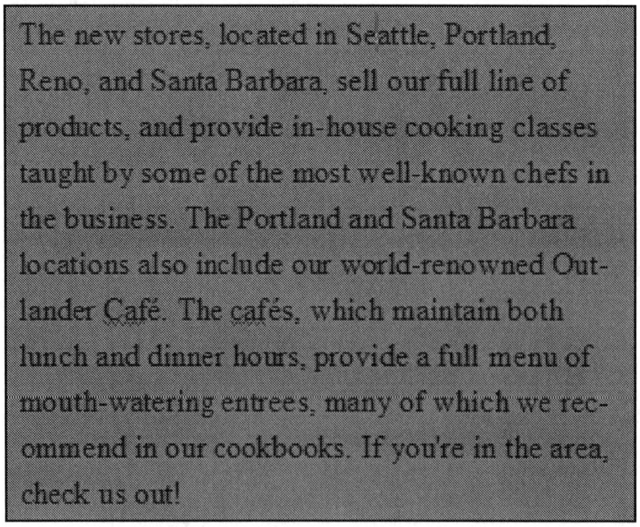

The new stores, located in Seattle, Portland, Reno, and Santa Barbara, sell our full line of products, and provide in-house cooking classes taught by some of the most well-known chefs in the business. The Portland and Santa Barbara locations also include our world-renowned Outlander Café. The cafés, which maintain both lunch and dinner hours, provide a full menu of mouth-watering entrees, many of which we recommend in our cookbooks. If you're in the area, check us out!

Exhibit 2-15: The word "café" with the symbol inserted in step 11

Review questions

1 What style is applied to text by default?

   Normal

2 You want to create a WordArt object that uses the same text as an existing headline. However, the headline contains some symbols, and you can't open the Symbol dialog box when the Edit WordArt dialog box is open. How can you create the WordArt object using the existing text?

   First select the text, and then open the Word Art Gallery. After you select a style, click OK to open the Edit WordArt dialog box—the text that you selected, along with any symbols or special characters, appears in the Text box.

3 What is a type mask?

   A technique wherein an image appears in the letters of text.

4 In order to align selected text to baseline guides, you have to check Align text to baseline guides. Where is this found?

   A In the Layout Guides dialog box

   B In the Paragraph dialog box

   C In the Format Text box dialog box

   D In the Page Setup dialog box

5 You want to insert a currency symbol, but you don't want to scroll through the entire list of symbols in the Symbol dialog box to find it. How can you quickly locate the currency symbols?

   To see a subset of available symbols in the Symbol dialog box, select it from the Subset list.

Unit 3

Long publications

Unit time: 15 minutes

Complete this unit, and you'll know how to:

A Create sections in a publication and format section page numbers.

B Create and use bookmarks.

Topic A: Sections

Explanation

Some publications, such as newspapers, contain multiple sections; in each section, the page numbering restarts at 1. Other publications, such as books, contain prefatory material and other sections such as appendixes. Often, these sections are numbered differently than the main section of the book. With Publisher, you can separate one publication into multiple sections, either retaining the page numbering or formatting each section's page numbers as you choose.

Creating sections

You can divide a publication into *sections* that have their own page numbering. By default, a publication has only one section.

To create a section:

1 If necessary, view the publication as single pages (rather than as a two-page spread).
2 Go to the page on which you want to begin a new section.
3 Choose Insert, Section to open the Section dialog box, shown in Exhibit 3-1.
4 Check Begin a section with this page.
5 Click OK.

If you're working with two-page spreads and you want the right-facing page in a spread to be the first page of a section (i.e., you want to begin a section in the middle of a spread), first view the publication as single pages by choosing View, Two-Page Spread. Otherwise, Publisher will use the left-facing page as the first page of the section.

Removing a section

To remove a section, go to the first page of the section and open the Section dialog box; clear Begin a section with this page, and click OK to remove the section.

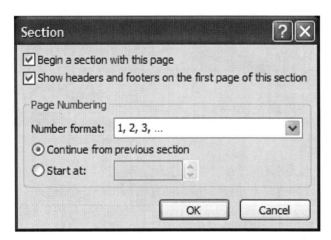

Exhibit 3-1: The Section dialog box

Do it!   **A-1:   Creating sections in a publication**

Here's how	Here's why
1 Open Sections.pub	From the current unit folder.
Save it as **My Sections**	
2 Choose **View, Two-Page Spread**	To view each page individually, rather than as a spread.
Go to page 3	Starting on page 3, you'll create a new section.
3 Choose **Insert, Section...**	To open the Section dialog box.
Check **Begin a section with this page**	
Click **OK**	
4 In the status bar, observe the page icons	

The space between pages 2 and 3 indicates a section division.

5 Create a new section that begins on page 5	Go to page 5. Then choose Insert, Section; check Begin a section with this page; and click OK.
6 Create a new section that begins on page 15	
7 Save the publication	

Section page numbers

Whenever you insert page numbers using the Insert, Page Numbers command, Publisher automatically formats page numbers starting at 1 and continuing consecutively through the publication. However, when you have multiple sections, you might want to format the page numbers differently. For example, many books contain a preface or introduction that is numbered with Roman numerals—"page 1" doesn't actually appear until several pages into the book.

You can tell Publisher how to format page numbers for different sections by using the Section dialog box, shown in Exhibit 3-1. Under Page Numbering, select a format from the Number format list. To restart the page numbering with the current section, select Start at, and edit the box, if necessary (the default value is 1).

Do it!

A-2:   Formatting section page numbers

Here's how	Here's why
1 Go to page 2	
Observe the table of contents	(Zoom in, if necessary.) The current page 3 should be page 1. The current pages 1 and 2 should be numbered with lower-case Roman numerals.
2 Go to page 1	
3 Open the Section dialog box	
From the Number format list, select **i, ii, iii,** ...	
Click **OK**	To close the dialog box.
4 At the bottom of the page, verify the result	(Zoom in, if necessary.) The page number is formatted as a lower-case Roman numeral.
On the status bar, observe the page icons	The pages are still numbered beginning with 1.
5 Go to page 3	
6 Open the Section dialog box	
Select **Start at**	
Edit the Start at box to read **1**	
Click **OK**	To close the dialog box.
7 At the bottom of the page, verify the result	This page is now numbered 1.
On the status bar, observe the page icons	The page numbering restarts with this section.
8 View the publication as a two-page spread	
9 Save the publication	

Point out that in many publications, the cover page and first few pages typically are not factored into the page numbering, as is the case with this publication.

⚠ Make sure that students are viewing the publication as single pages, rather than as a two-page spread.

Topic B: Bookmarks

Explanation

You can use a *bookmark* to mark a location in a publication, which you can then navigate to directly by clicking the associated bookmark entry in the Bookmark dialog box. You can add bookmarks to specific locations in a publication.

Adding bookmarks

Bookmarks can help in locating specific sections of a publication without having to search for them. Bookmarks are particularly useful when you're working in a large publication. To add a bookmark:

1   Go to the page where you want to add the bookmark.
2   On the Object toolbar, click the Bookmark button to open the Bookmark dialog box, shown in Exhibit 3-2.
3   In the Bookmark name box, enter a name for the bookmark.
4   Click Add to add the bookmark.

Exhibit 3-2: The Bookmark dialog box

Do it!

B-1:   Adding bookmarks

Here's how	Here's why
1 Go to page i	
2 On the Objects toolbar, click [icon]	(The Bookmark button.) To open the Bookmark dialog box.
In the Bookmark name box, type **Andrews letter**	
Click **Add**	[icon]
	To insert a bookmark, which appears as an icon in the center of the page.
3 Move the bookmark icon to the top-left page margin	
4 On page ii, create a bookmark named **Contents**	Go to page 2. On the Objects toolbar, click the Bookmark button. Name the bookmark Contents, and click Add.
5 Move the bookmark icon to the top-left page margin	
6 On page 1, create a bookmark named **Spice history**	
7 On page 2, create a bookmark named **The spice trade**	
8 Save the publication	

Locating bookmarks

Explanation

After you've added bookmarks to a publication, you can use the Bookmark dialog box to navigate directly to any bookmark. To navigate to a bookmark:

1 On the Objects toolbar, click the Bookmark button to open the Bookmark dialog box.
2 Under Bookmark name, select a bookmark.
3 Click Go To.

Do it!

B-2: Navigating to a bookmark

Here's how	Here's why
1 Open the Bookmark dialog box	On the Objects toolbar, click the Bookmark button.
2 Next to Sort by, select **Location**	To sort the bookmark names by their location in the publication, rather than by their names.
3 From the Bookmark name list, select **Andrews letter**	
Click **Go To**	Publisher moves to the bookmark and zooms to 100%.
4 Navigate to the other bookmarks	In the Bookmark dialog box, select the name of the bookmark, then click Go To.
5 Click **Cancel**	To close the dialog box.
6 Save the publication	

Deleting bookmarks

Explanation

When you want to delete a bookmark, select it in the Bookmark dialog box and then click Delete. You will not be prompted to confirm the deletion. If you mistakenly delete a bookmark, you'll have to create it again.

Do it!

B-3: Deleting a bookmark

Here's how	Here's why
1 Open the Bookmark dialog box	
2 From the Bookmark name list, select **The spice trade**	
Click **Delete**	To delete the bookmark and close the dialog box.
3 Save and close the publication	

Unit summary: Long publications

Topic A

In this topic, you learned how to insert **sections** in a publication, and format **section page numbers**.

Topic B

In this topic, you learned how to use **bookmarks**. You learned how to insert bookmarks, navigate to bookmarks, and delete bookmarks.

Independent practice activity

In this activity, you'll insert a section in a publication and format each section's page numbers. Then you'll add bookmarks.

1 Open Practice sections.pub (from the current unit folder), and save it as **My Practice sections**.

2 Create a new section beginning on page 5. (*Hint*: To begin a section on page 5, you'll have to view the document as single pages, rather than as a two-page spread.)

3 Format the section page numbering so that pages 1-4 are numbered with lower-case Roman numerals and the numbering on page 5 begins with 1. The numbering should be as follows: i, ii, iii, iv, 1, 2, 3, 4.

4 Create bookmarks for the Bay Leaves and Cilantro/Coriander subheadings on page 1.

5 Save and close the publication.

Review questions

1 You want to begin a new section on the right-facing page of a double-page spread. What must you do first?

To start a new section in the middle of a spread, you must first view the publication as single pages.

2 Which dialog box do you use to format section page numbers?

A The Insert Page dialog box

B The Section dialog box

C The Page Numbers dialog box

D The Page Setup dialog box

3 Which of the following can you bookmark? (Select one.)

A Text boxes

B Pictures

C Pages

D Any location on a layout

4 How do you navigate to a bookmark?

On the Objects toolbar, click the Bookmark button to open the Bookmark dialog box. Under Bookmark name, select a bookmark. Click Go To.

5 How do you delete a bookmark?

Select the bookmark in the Bookmark dialog box and then click Delete.

U n i t   4

Mail merge

Unit time: 60 minutes

Complete this unit, and you'll know how to:

A Create a recipient list for a mail merge.

B Prepare mailing labels.

C Begin a mail merge by connecting to a recipient list, and sort and filter the recipient list.

D Add mail merge fields to a publication.

E Create a merged publication.

Topic A: Recipient lists

Explanation

If you mail your publications, you're likely to have a recipient list. A *recipient list* is a list of names and addresses stored in an external file that can be used in Publisher to complete a mail merge. Using a recipient list can save you time because Publisher can store the address information and use it to quickly create customized publications or mailing labels.

Creating a recipient list

When you're using mail merge, you might already have the recipient list data in an external source, such as an Excel spreadsheet or a Microsoft Word table. Having an existing data source is helpful, but there might be occasions when you need to create a recipient list during the mail merge process.

To create a recipient list:

1. Choose Tools, Mailings and Catalogs, Create Address List. The New Address List dialog box opens, as shown in Exhibit 4-1.
2. Click Customize Columns to add or delete fields, if necessary.
3. Enter the record data for each recipient in the New Address List dialog box.
4. Click OK, and save the data source.

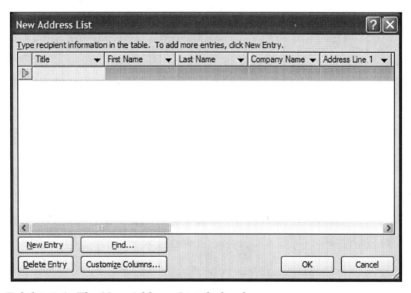

Exhibit 4-1: The New Address List dialog box

Do it!

A-1:   Creating a recipient list

Here's how	Here's why
Tell students that they're just creating a recipient list, so they don't have to save the publication. 1 Open a new, blank publication	If necessary.
2 Choose **Tools,** **Mailings and Catalogs,** **Create Address List...**	To open the New Address List dialog box.
Point out that they don't need all the fields, so they'll customize the field list. 3 Click **Customize Columns**	
	To open the Customize Address List dialog box, which you can use to add or delete fields.
Click **Delete**	To delete the selected Title field. You're prompted to confirm the deletion.
Click **Yes**	
4 From the Field Names list, select **Company Name**	You'll send the brochure to Outlander customers, so you don't need the Company Name field.
Delete the field name	
5 Delete these fields: Address Line 2, Country or Region, Home Phone, Work Phone, and E-mail Address	If you need any additional fields, you could click Add to insert them now. You could also edit the name of a field by clicking Rename.
Click **OK**	To close the Customize Address List box.
To view the Zip Code field, they can press tab after entering data in the State field, or use the horizontal scrollbar at the bottom of the dialog box. 6 Enter the following data: **Rod Yun** **8201 Broadleaf Rd** **Chicago, IL 60611**	

Type recipient information in the table. To add more entries, click New Entry.

▼	Last Name	▼	Address Line 1	▼	City	▼	State	▼	ZIP Code	▼
	Yun		8201 Broadleaf Rd		Chicago		IL		60611	

TIPS ✓ *Students can also press Tab to add a new row for the next entry.*

7	Click **New Entry**	To complete the first address list entry, and add a new row for the next entry.

Enter the following data:
Tracy McGarvey
1191 Holmes Pkwy
Detroit, MI 48205

Type recipient information in the table. To add more entries, click New Entry.

▼	Last Name ▼	Address Line 1 ▼	City ▼	State ▼	ZIP Code ▼
	Yun	8201 Broadleaf Rd	Chicago	IL	60611
	McGarvey	1191 Holmes Pkwy	Detroit	MI	48205

8	After entering the zip code, press TAB	To create another new entry.

9	Enter the following data: **Tanya Poole** **72 Lee St** **Orlando, FL 32811**	

10	Click **OK**	To open the Save Address List dialog box.
	Navigate to the current unit folder	
	In the File name box, enter **My data source**	In the Save as type list, Microsoft Office Address Lists is selected. The data source will be saved as a Microsoft Office Address List.
	Click **Save**	To save the new address list.

Topic B: Mailing labels

Explanation

You can use the mail merge feature to create mailing labels using the data from a recipients list. After creating mailing labels, you can print them onto labels that you can affix to envelopes.

Preparing mailing labels

Publisher includes a number of templates for labels that correspond to standard Avery label sheets.

To use a mailing label template:

1 Open a new publication.
2 In the Format Publication pane, click Change Template to open the Change Template dialog box.
3 From the list, select Labels.
4 Select the desired label style.
5 Click OK.

Do it!

B-1:   Preparing mailing labels

Here's how	Here's why
1 Save the current blank publication as **My mail merge**	In the current unit folder.
2 In the Format Publication pane, click **Change Template**	To open the Change Template dialog box.
3 From the list on the left side, select **Labels**	
Under Classic Designs, select **Batik (Avery 5160)**	
Click **OK**	A message appears, indicating that the selected template will change the default layout of the current publication.
Select **Apply template to the current publication**	
Click **OK**	To create the label template. Only one label is shown, but Publisher will create a page with multiple labels, according to which style you've selected.
4 Delete the text in the text box	You'll insert fields for a mail merge in the text box.
5 Save the publication	

Topic C: The Mail Merge pane

Explanation

The Mail Merge pane guides you through the steps for completing a mail merge, including selecting or creating a recipient list, preparing the publication by inserting mail merge fields, and creating a merged publication.

Attaching a recipient list

You can either create a new recipient list or attach an existing one. If you have an existing document that contains a list of recipients, such as a Word table or an Excel spreadsheet, you can specify that document as your recipient list.

To specify a recipients list:

1 Open or create the starting publication.

2 Open the Mail Merge pane, shown in Exhibit 4-2.

3 Under Create recipient list, select the desired option: use an existing list, select from your Outlook Contacts, or create a new list.

4 Click Next: Create or connect to a recipient list:

- If you selected Use an existing list, the Select Data Source dialog box opens. Select the data source and click Open.

- If you selected Select from Outlook Contacts, the Select Contacts dialog box opens. (Or, if you haven't created any contacts in Outlook, you're prompted to do so.)

- If you selected Type a new list, the New Address List dialog box opens.

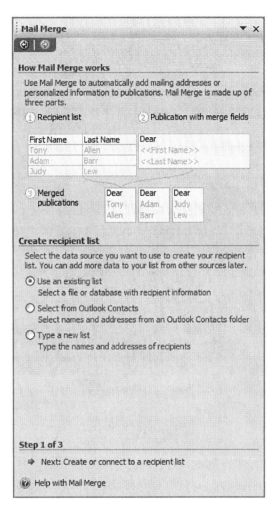

Exhibit 4-2: The Mail Merge pane

Do it!

C-1:   Beginning a mail merge

Here's how	Here's why
1 Open the Mail Merge pane	Under Create recipient list, Use an existing list is selected by default.
2 Under Step 1 of 3, click **Next: Create or connect to a recipient list**	(At the bottom of the pane.) To open the Select Data Source dialog box.
Navigate to the current unit folder	
3 Select **My data source**	This is the recipient list that you created.
4 Click **Open**	To open the Mail Merge Recipients dialog box.

Tell students to leave the dialog box open for the next activity.

Sorting records

Explanation

Before you print your form letters, you might want to sort the letters based on specific merge field data. For example, you might need to print the form letters in alphabetical order by last name. You can do this by sorting the records in the data source.

After you've selected a data source, either the Mail Merge Recipients dialog box (shown in Exhibit 4-3) or the New Address List dialog box opens, depending on which option you selected. You also can open the Mail Merge Recipients dialog box to sort records by choosing Tools, Mailings and Catalogs, Edit Address List.

To sort records:

1 Open the Mail Merge Recipients dialog box.

2 Under Refine recipient list, click Sort to open the Filter and Sort dialog box.

3 From the Sort by list, select the field by which you want to sort the recipients.

4 Select either Ascending or Descending.

5 Click OK to close the Filter and Sort dialog box.

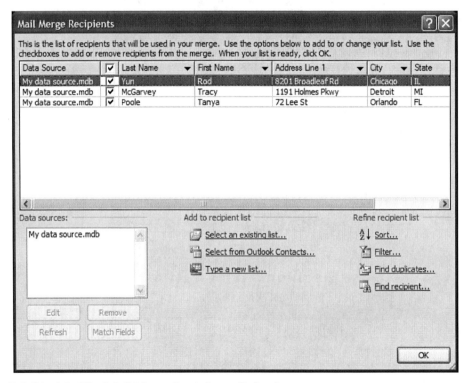

Exhibit 4-3: The Mail Merge Recipients dialog box

Do it!

C-2: Sorting recipients

Tell students that if the dialog box isn't open, they can open it by opening the Mail Merge pane; in step 2, click Edit recipient list.

Here's how	Here's why
1 Observe the order of the names in the recipient list	(In the Mail Merge Recipients dialog box.) They're not currently sorted—they're listed in the order in which you entered them.
2 Under Refine recipient list, click **Sort...**	To open the Filter and Sort dialog box.
3 From the Sort by list, select **Last Name**	The Ascending option is selected by default.
Click **OK**	To close the Filter and Sort dialog box. The records are sorted by last name in ascending order.

Tell students to leave the dialog box open for the next activity.

Filtering records

Either during or after the mail merge process, you might decide to print only letters for a specific group of recipients. For example, you might want to send flyers to recipients who live in a particular city. To print only a subset of your recipients, you can filter out the unwanted records.

To filter records in a data source:

1 Open the Mail Merge Recipients dialog box.
2 Click Filter to open the Filter and Sort dialog box.
3 Specify the criteria for filtering the records, and click OK.

The difference between sorting and filtering is that when you sort, all records are displayed according to the sort condition. For example, if you sort by state in ascending order, all records are listed from Alabama to Wyoming. When you apply a filter, only those records that meet the filtering condition are displayed. For example, if you apply a filter for Illinois, only those records with Illinois in the State field will be displayed.

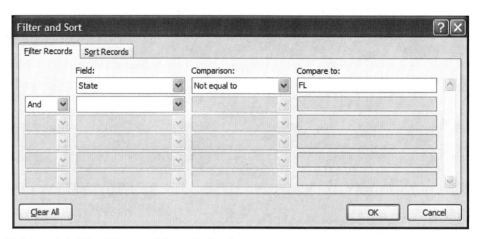

Exhibit 4-4: The Filter and Sort dialog box

C-3:   Filtering recipients

Here's how	Here's why
1 Under Refine recipient list, click **Filter...**	(In the Mail Merge Recipients dialog box.) You'll create a filter to eliminate customers from Florida.
2 From the Field list, select **State**	In the Comparison list, Equal to is selected.
From the Comparison list, select **Not equal to**	
In the Compare to box, enter **FL**	To specify a value for comparison.
3 Click **OK**	Only two records now appear in the dialog box.
4 Click **OK**	To close the dialog box and move to step 2 in the Mail Merge pane.

Topic D: Mail merge fields

Explanation

After you've selected a recipient list, step 2 of the mail merge process is to insert selected merge fields in the publication. A *merge field* is a placeholder for data that can change. For example, you use the First name field to insert a recipient's first name from each record set.

Adding merge fields

In step 2 of the mail merge process, the Mail Merge pane appears as shown in Exhibit 4-5. From here, you can insert and preview recipient information, edit the recipient list, and insert additional fields. For example, if you're creating a form letter, you could click Address block to open the Insert Address Block dialog box, which you could use to insert the recipient's full name. All the fields you'll need for mailing labels, however, are shown under Prepare your publication.

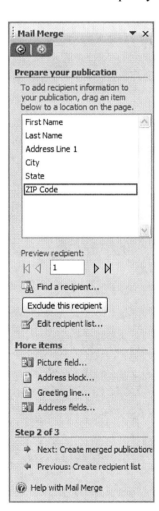

Exhibit 4-5: Step 2 in the Mail Merge pane

To insert a merge field:

1 Open the Mail Merge pane, and go to step 2.

2 Click or drag to insert the desired fields from the list:

- Drag the field to a blank area of the layout to create a new text box containing the field.

- Drag the field to an existing text box to insert the field.

- Place the insertion point where you want the field and then click the field in the Mail Merge task pane.

In the publication, selected fields appear as shown in Exhibit 4-6. When not selected, they display the associated information from the record set, but the text still appears with the blue, dotted underlining.

«First_Name» «Last_Name»
«Address_Line 1»
«City» «State» «ZIP Code»

Exhibit 4-6: Selected fields

Modifying fields

After inserting a merge field, you can modify the information associated with it by pointing to it and clicking the Merge Field icon, shown in Exhibit 4-7. From the list that appears, select Edit Recipient List to open the Mail Merge Recipients dialog box.

«First_Name»

Exhibit 4-7: The Merge Field icon

Do it!

D-1:   Adding mail merge fields to a publication

Here's how	Here's why
1 Observe the list under Prepare your publication	(In the Mail Merge pane.) The list includes the fields that you specified in the Customize Address List dialog box.
2 From the list, drag **First Name** into the text box on the page	To insert the First Name field.
Press (SPACEBAR)	To insert a space after the First Name field.
3 In the Mail Merge pane, click **Last Name**	To insert the field in the text box.
Press (↵ ENTER)	To create a new line on the mailing label.
4 In the Mail Merge pane, click **Address Line 1**	
Press (↵ ENTER)	
5 Insert the City field	In the Mail Merge pane, click City.
Press (SPACEBAR)	
6 Insert the State field	
Press (SPACEBAR)	
7 Insert the ZIP Code field	
8 In the Mail Merge pane, under Preview recipient, click ▷	(The Next button.) To see the information for the second record in the publication.
Click ◁	(The Previous button.) To preview the first record.
9 Save the publication	

Tell students that they can click fields or drag them, whichever they prefer.

Topic E: Merged publications

Explanation

The final step in the mail merge process is creating the merged publication. Publisher creates one publication with a separate section for each record set.

Creating a merged publication

After you've inserted the desired merge fields and formatted them, the final step is to create the merged publication. To do so, click Next: Create merged publication (in the Mail Merge pane). The Mail Merge pane will display step 3, as shown in Exhibit 4-8. From here, select how you want to create the merged publication:

- Click Print to open the Print dialog box.
- Click Print Preview to preview the printed pages.
- Click Merge to a new publication to create a new publication with the merged data.
- Click Add to existing publication to open the Open Publication dialog box, from which you can select an existing publication to add the merged publication to.

When you merge the publication, publisher creates separate copies of the publication for each record set. For example, if you create a new publication that contains records for 10 recipients, Publisher creates 10 copies of the publication, each in its own section, and each containing one record set.

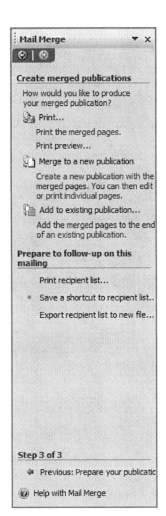

Exhibit 4-8: Step 3 in the Mail Merge pane

Do it!   **E-1:   Completing a mail merge**

Here's how	Here's why
1 In the Mail Merge pane, click **Next: Create merged publications**	To move to step 3 of the mail merge.
2 Under Create merged publications, click **Merge to a new publication**	To create a new publication that includes the merged pages.
3 Observe the label	The first column contains the information from the first record set.
4 Observe the page icons	There are two sections. The second section is a duplicate of the publication that contains the information from the second record set.
5 Go to page 2	
6 On the Standard toolbar, click	(The Print Preview button.) To preview how the printed page will appear. Use the preview to verify that you're using the correct label design.
On the toolbar, click **Close**	To close the preview and return to the layout view.
7 Save the publication as **Merged brochure**	In the current unit folder.
8 Close the publication	
9 Save and close the My mail merge publication	

Unit summary: Mail merge

Topic A   In this topic, you learned how to create a **recipient list** for a mail merge.

Topic B   In this topic, you created a publication using a **label template** to prepare it for a mail merge.

Topic C   In this topic, you started a **mail merge** by using the Mail Merge pane. Then you learned how to **sort** and **filter** a recipient list by using the Filter and Sort dialog box.

Topic D   In this topic, you learned how to add **mail merge fields** to a publication.

Topic E   In this topic, you completed a mail merge by creating a **merged publication**.

Independent practice activity

In this activity, you'll create a new recipient list and sort it. Then you'll insert mail merge fields on a layout and create a merged publication.

Limited-run mail merge

Typically, you'll use mail merge to create labels or form letters, rather than full-color publications such as newsletters. In this case, however, you need to send a few newsletters to some clients who were left off of a previous printing. You'll merge their information directly into the publication and print the newsletters in house.

1 Open Practice mail merge.pub (from the current unit folder), and save it as **My Practice mail merge**.

2 Go to page 6.

3 Open the Mail Merge pane and begin creating a new recipient list.

4 In the New Address List dialog box, enter the following recipients:

- **Andrew James, 1074 4th St, Astoria, OR 97103**
- **Susan Lodge, 2265 Saguaro St, Phoenix, AZ 85001**
- **William Fox, 8225 E Mountain Hwy, Colorado Springs, CO 80901**

5 Delete the unnecessary columns from the New Address List dialog box.

6 Save the address list in the current unit folder as **Practice list**.

7 Sort the list by ZIP code.

8 Create a new text box, and add the address fields to it. (*Hint*: Remember to insert spaces where appropriate to separate fields.)

9 Merge the recipient data to a new publication, and save it as **My practice mailing**.

10 Save and close all open publications.

Review questions

1 How do you open the New Address List dialog box to begin creating a new recipient list for a mail merge?

   Choose Tools, Mailings and Catalogs, Create Address List.

2 True or false? You can either create a new recipient list or attach an existing one

   True. If you have an existing document that contains a list of recipients, such as a Word table or an Excel spreadsheet, you can specify that document as your recipient list.

3 How do you sort and filter a recipient list?

   Open the Mail Merge Recipients dialog box, then, under Refine recipient list, click Sort to open the Filter and Sort dialog box.

4 Describe the three methods for inserting a merge field from the Mail Merge pane.

   • *Drag the field to a blank area of the layout to create a new text box containing the field.*

   • *Drag the field to an existing text box to insert the field.*

   • *Place the insertion point where you want the field and then click the field in the Mail Merge pane.*

5 For a mail merge, your recipient list contains 37 record sets. In the final step, you choose to merge the data to a new publication. How many sections (i.e., copies of the original publication) will the new publication contain?

   37—one for each record set in the recipient list.

Unit 5

Interactive forms

Unit time: 60 minutes

Complete this unit, and you'll know how to:

A Create a Web publication, a Web form, and insert and modify form elements.

B Set form properties and labels.

Topic A: Web forms

Explanation   Publisher is primarily a print publication tool, but you can also use it to design and create Web pages. You can even create forms to help make your Web site interactive. Forms allow users to send information to a site owner. For example, a visitor to a site could use a form to create an account, make a purchase, or request information.

Converting to a Web publication

When you're working with a print publication, the Web Tools toolbar—which contains the tools you'll need to create a form—is not available. If you want to create a Web form based on a print publication, you must first convert the publication to a Web publication. Choose File, Convert to Web Publication. A brief wizard appears, asking you to specify some preferences. You can also convert a Web publication to a print publication by choosing File, Convert to Print Publication.

Forms

A form can contain text boxes, check boxes, and other form elements that enable a user to specify choices or enter information. When finished, a user typically presses a Submit button. The Submit button can launch a script that sends the user's information to the Web server, where it's processed by a database application.

The Web Tools toolbar

When you're working with a Web publication, the Web Tools toolbar is displayed, as shown in Exhibit 5-1. The toolbar contains buttons for working with Web sites, including the Form Control button, which you can use to insert form elements.

Exhibit 5-1: The Web Tools toolbar

The following table lists the buttons available on the Web Tools toolbar.

Button	Icon	Description
Publish to the Web		Opens the Publish to the Web dialog box.
Web Page Preview		Opens the Web page in your default browser.
Insert Hyperlink		Opens the Insert Hyperlink dialog box when text or a picture is selected.
Hot Spot		Changes the cursor to a crosshair, which you can drag to create a hot spot. A *hot spot* is an area on the page that acts as a hyperlink.
Navigation Bar		Opens the Design Gallery dialog box, with the Navigation Bars section active.

Button	Icon	Description
Rename		Opens the Web Page Options dialog box, in which you can rename the Web page by editing the Page title box.
Background		Opens the Background task pane, which you can use to apply a background color or design to your Web page.
Background Sound		Opens the Web Page Options dialog box, which you can use to insert a background sound (for example, a music file) on your Web page. To do so, under Background sound, click Browse and select the file.
Form Control		Displays a list of options for inserting form elements.
Bookmark		Opens the Bookmark dialog box.
HTML Code Fragment		Opens the Edit HTML Code Fragment dialog box, in which you can enter HTML code.
Web Site Options		Opens the Options dialog box, with the Web tab active.
Web Page Options		Opens the Web Page Options dialog box.

The following table lists the form element options that appear when you click the Form Control button.

Form element	Description
Textbox	Accepts a single word or short phrase, such as a name or address.
Text Area	Accepts longer text entries, such as a question, comment, or a description of a problem.
Checkbox	Selects multiple items.
Option Button	Selects only one item from a list of items.
List Box	Displays a list from which the user can select one or more items.
Submit	Submits a completed form, or clears all entries so that a user can begin again.

Do it! **A-1: Converting a print publication to a Web publication**

Here's how	Here's why
1 Open Web form.pub	From the current unit folder.
Save it as **My Web form**	(In the Current unit folder.) This is a print publication that contains a form layout that you'll use on the Outlander Web site. However, to access the Web Tools toolbar, you need to convert it to a Web publication.
2 Choose **File**, **Convert to Web Publication**	The Convert to Web publication dialog box appears.
Select the second option	The option that reads, "No, do not save my print publication before converting it to a Web publication."
Click **Next**	
Select the second option	You don't need a navigation bar for this page.
Click **Finish**	To convert the publication. The Web Tools toolbar is now visible.
3 On the Web Tools toolbar, click [icon]	
	(The Form Control button.) To view the available form elements.
Move the pointer away from the toolbar	To hide the list.
4 Save the publication	If necessary, choose My Web form in the current unit folder.

Textboxes and text areas

Explanation

Textboxes are intended for short alphanumeric entries, usually on a single line. For example, if you want to create a box for users to enter their name, you'd use a textbox. You can adjust the width of a textbox, but not the height.

A *text area* allows long entries or multiple lines of text. They're often used to collect user comments or questions that don't fit in a textbox. You can adjust both the width and height of a text area.

To insert an inline textbox or a text area, place the insertion point on the page and click the Form Control button. Then, select either Textbox or Text Area.

Do it!

A-2: Inserting text input fields

Here's how	Here's why
1 Place the insertion point as shown	**Personal information** First name:
2 On the Web Tools toolbar, click 🖼️	(The Form Control button.) A menu appears.
Select **Textbox**	A textbox appears at the insertion point. The spacing might look off-center, but it will display correctly in a browser.
3 Resize the textbox as shown	**Personal information** First name:
	(Drag the center right handle to the right.) To make the textbox wide enough to capture long names.
4 Press ⌨CTRL + C	To copy the textbox.
⌨CTRL + V	To paste the textbox. Making copies of textboxes can help ensure that you're using input fields of equal size.
5 Drag the copied textbox next to the Last name prompt	
6 Create duplicate textboxes for the Email, Address and Address 2 prompts	Press Ctrl+V three times, and then drag each textbox next to the prompts.

⚠️ *If students make the textbox too wide, it will wrap to a second line. Tell them to change the width as necessary.*

⚠️ *The text box must be selected before they can copy it.*

7   Place the insertion point next to the Phone prompt

On the Web Tools toolbar, click ▣

Select **Textbox**   To insert a new textbox with the default size. This input field is collecting phone numbers, which won't require as long a textbox as the others. The default size should suffice.

8   Select the textbox and press
    CTRL + C   To copy the textbox.

    CTRL + V three times   To insert three copies of the textbox.

Tell them they'll create a different type of input field for the Country prompt later.

Drag the duplicates next to the City, State, and ZIP prompts   The textboxes don't need to line up perfectly.

9   Place the insertion point as shown

> Would you prefer the information:
>   In printed form   Delivered electronically
>
> Comments or questions:
> |

From the From Control list, select **Text Area**

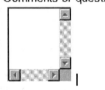

To insert a text area field.

Tell students to click the field, and then drag the lower-right corner handle to resize the text area's height and width.

Resize the text area as shown

10 Save the publication   You'll come back to these input fields a bit later.

List boxes

Explanation

List boxes allow a user to select one or more items from a list of pre-defined items. A list box displays a fixed number of rows. If there are more items in a list than it can display due to its size, a scroll bar appears to allow the user to access all items. If you reduce a list box's height so that only one item appears, the entire list appears when a user clicks the list, as shown in the example on the right in Exhibit 5-2.

A list box with a fixed height.

A list box resized to show only one item. When clicked, a menu appears to display the entire list.

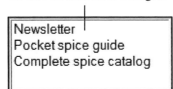

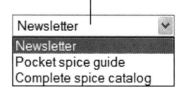

Exhibit 5-2: List boxes

To insert a list box:

1 Place the insertion point where you want to insert the list box. On the Web Tools toolbar, click the Form Control button, and select List Box.

2 Double-click the list box to open the List Box Properties dialog box, shown in Exhibit 5-3.

3 Edit the label in the "Return data with this label" box.

4 Add, modify, or remove items from the list as necessary.

5 To allow a user to select more than one item from a list, check "User can select more than one item". (On a Windows PC, a user can select more than one item by holding Ctrl and clicking the items in the list; on a Mac, a user can do this by holding Command and clicking the items.)

6 If there's a default item for this list (for example, the default value might be "Select an item from the list"), select it and click Modify; in the Add/Modify List Box Item dialog box, select Selected.

Exhibit 5-3: The List Box Properties dialog box

Do it!

A-3: Creating a list box

Here's how	Here's why
1 Place the insertion point next to the Country prompt	
From the Form Control list, select **List Box**	To insert a list box. By default, a new list box contains three items, and all are visible.
2 Reduce the list box as shown	
	Drag the top resize handle as far down as it will go, so that only one item appears.
3 Double-click the list box	To open the List Box Properties dialog box. In the Appearance list, the first item is selected.
4 Click **Modify**	To open the Add/Modify List Box Item dialog box.
Type **United States**	In the Item box.
Under Show item as, verify that Selected is selected	This item is the default selection for this list box.
Click **OK**	To close the dialog box and return to the List Box Properties dialog box.
5 In the Appearance list, select **Item Two**	
Click **Modify**	
Type **Canada**, and click **OK**	
6 Modify the third item to read **Mexico**	
7 Click **OK**	To close the List Box Properties dialog box.

Most of Outlander Spices' customers are located in the United States, so this is a logical default selection.

Tell students to drag the Web Tools toolbar out of the way, if necessary.

8 Insert a list box in the area shown

Your request

Check the items that you're interested in:
Cooking   Baking

Which publication(s) would you like to rec

| Item One |
| Item Two |
| Item Three |

Would you prefer the information:
In printed form   Delivered electronically

Double-click the list box — To open the List Box Properties dialog box.

9 Click **Modify** — To modify the first item.

Type **Newsletter**

Under Show item as, select **Not selected** — In this list box, you don't want any of the items to be selected by default.

Click **OK** — To close the dialog box.

10 Make the second and third items read **Pocket spice guide** and **Complete spice catalog**

If they already closed the dialog box, tell them to double-click it again.

11 In the List Box Properties dialog box, check **User can select more than one item** — So that a user can select more than one item.

Click **OK** — To close the dialog box.

12 Save the publication

Checkboxes and option buttons

Explanation

Checkboxes allow a user to select one or more items. For example, if you have a variety of items, such as a newsletter, coupons, promotions, and an annual report, you could make those items individual checkboxes and users could select which items they're interested in. To insert a checkbox, place the insertion point, click the Form Control button, and select Checkbox. (If you insert a checkbox without placing the insertion point, Publisher creates a checkbox with a space for a label.)

Option buttons, which are also known as radio buttons, are typically grouped to allow only one selection, so that clicking one option button clears any other selection in that group. For example, when asking users to specify their gender, you'd want to use option buttons instead of checkboxes because the nature of the data is mutually exclusive; a user can only be male or female.

To insert an option button, place the insertion point, click the Form Control button, and select Option Button.

Do it!

A-4: Inserting checkboxes and option buttons

Here's how	Here's why
1 Place the insertion point as shown	**Your request** Check the items that yo Cooking Baking
	You'll insert checkboxes so that users can select one or both of the items.
From the Form Control list, select **Checkbox**	To insert a checkbox.
2 Insert a checkbox before the word Baking	First, place the insertion point. Then, from the Form Control list, select Checkbox.
3 Place the insertion point as shown	Would you prefer [n printed form
	You'll insert option buttons so that users can select only one of the items listed.
From the Form Control list, select **Option Button**	To insert an option button.
4 Insert an option button before "Delivered electronically"	First, place the insertion point. Then, from the Form Control list, select Option Button.
5 Save the publication	

Submit and reset buttons

Explanation

A form needs a submit button so that users can send their data to your Web server. A *submit button* is linked to a script that transmits the values entered into the input fields to the database or Web server where the information is processed. A *reset button* is an optional button you can add to a form to enable users to clear all their input field values and start over again.

To add a button to a form:

1   On the Web Tools toolbar, click the Form Control button and select Submit to open the Command Button Properties dialog box, shown in Exhibit 5-4.

2   Select either Reset or Submit.

3   Clear "Button text is same as button type" to edit the Button text box.

4   Click OK.

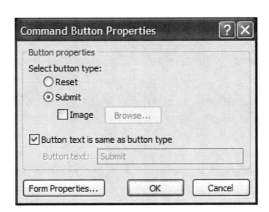

Exhibit 5-4: The Command Button Properties dialog box

Do it!

A-5:   Inserting submit and reset buttons

Remind students that the scratch area is the gray area outside the page.

Here's how	Here's why
1 Click the scratch area	(To deselect all items on the page.) You'll insert buttons so that users can submit the information they've entered, or reset the form, clearing the information they've entered.
2 From the Form Control list, select **Submit**	To open the Command Button Properties dialog box.
Click **OK**	To create a submit button.
3 Drag the button to the position shown	Comments or questions:

[text area with Submit button]

Your submit button should be in a logical, intuitive location relative to the form. Typically, the best place for a submit button is after the last input field. |
4 From the form Control list, select **Submit**	To open the Command Button Properties dialog box.
Select **Reset**	
Clear **Button text is same as button type**	
Edit the Button text box to read **Start over**	
5 Click **OK**	To create the reset button.

6 Drag the button to the position
    shown

Comments or questions:

Start over   Submit

7 Save the publication

Topic B: Form settings

Explanation

When you create a Web form, you need to specify how the data will be stored. You can save it in a file on your Web server, e-mail it, or use a program provided by your Internet service provider (ISP). You can also label form elements so that a database or other program can organize the data.

Form properties

After you've added a form element, you can double-click it to open its dialog box. In each dialog box, you can click Form Properties to open the Form Properties dialog box, shown in Exhibit 5-5. Using the settings in this dialog box, you can choose how the data entered by a user will be processed. For some options, you'll need to use a Web host that supports Microsoft FrontPage server extensions. The following table describes the three methods for retrieving data from a form in Publisher.

Data retrieval method	Description
Save the data in a file on my Web server	Select this option to save the data to an online database in either HTML or text format. Consult your Web host to determine the best method for formatting the data. Requires Microsoft FrontPage server extensions (version 2.0 or higher).
Send data to me in e-mail	Select this option to send the data in an e-mail, which you specify, with a subject line that you choose. Requires Microsoft FrontPage98 server extensions (version 3.0 or higher).
Use a program from my ISP	Select this option if your ISP uses a program or script to process form data. Consult your ISP or Web host for this information.

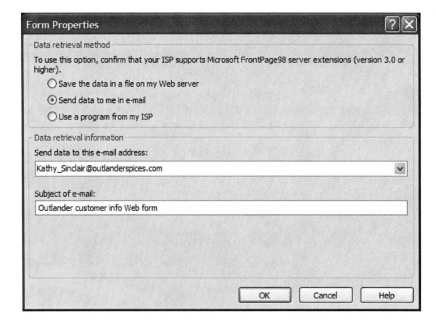

Exhibit 5-5: The Form Properties dialog box

Do it!

B-1: Sending form data via e-mail

Here's how	Here's why
1 Double-click any one of the form elements you've inserted	
In the dialog box, click **Form Properties**	To open the Form Properties dialog box.
2 Select **Send data to me in e-mail**	
3 In the first box, enter **<Your_Name>@outlander spices.com**	
4 Edit the second box to read **Outlander customer info**	
5 Click **OK**	To close the Form Properties dialog box. This form setting is automatically applied to every input field in the form.
Click **OK**	To close the dialog box.
6 Save the publication	

Tell students that typically, user feedback and data should be processed on a server and stored in a database.

Form labels

Explanation

Each form element's dialog box contains a "Return data with this label" box. This label is a vital part of a form's functionality because it tells the script or program that processes the data which category the data belongs to. For example, you should give a First Name textbox a label like Fname or FirstName. The label you choose must match its corresponding field in a database. If a database already exists, you need to make sure your labels match precisely with their corresponding fields in the database.

By default, Publisher labels each field according to the type of field it is, followed by a number representing the number of unique fields currently in the form. For example, if you create a new form and insert a list box, Publisher gives it the label "LIST_BOX_1". (Notice that underscore characters are used. Spaces are not allowed in label names, so if you need to separate words, use an underscore character.)

Always make sure your label names are meaningful and appropriate to the type of data the field is used for. It often makes sense to make a label the same or similar to its text prompt. For example, if you create a list box that allows a user to select their country of origin, a logical label and database field name would be "Country".

Preventing errors with form labels

Every input field in a form must be uniquely labeled. When you make copies of form input fields, as you did in Activity A-2, the labels remain the same, based on the copied label. For example, if you copy a textbox labeled Text_1 and paste it four times, you'll have five textboxes with the same label. Therefore, when you make copies of input fields, it's critical that you update their labels appropriately to ensure that your form submits valid data to your database.

Checkbox and option button labels

Checkboxes and option buttons have an additional setting for data processing. For checkboxes, you typically want to allow a user to select as many (or as few) checkboxes as they'd like. To do so, give each checkbox a unique value in the "Return data with this label" box. This is the category in which the data will be placed. The label for each checkbox should be unique. The Checkbox value box indicates the value returned by the form in that category. For example, the settings shown in Exhibit 5-6 would return the value Cooking="Yes" if a user selects that checkbox and submits the form.

On the other hand, when you use option buttons, you typically want a user to select only one item from a related group of options. To do so, make the "Return data with this label" box the same for every option button that you want to include in a group. A user will only be able to select one of the option buttons in such a group. The Option button value box, however, should be unique for each option button. For example, the settings shown in Exhibit 5-7 would return the value SendInfo="Printed" if a user selects that option button and submits the form.

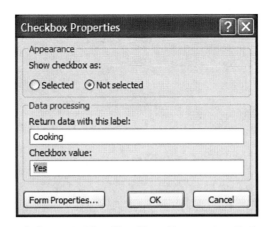

Exhibit 5-6: The Checkbox Properties dialog box

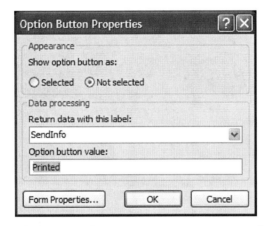

Exhibit 5-7: The Option Button Properties dialog box

Do it!

B-2: Labeling form elements

Here's how	Here's why
1 Double-click the textbox next to the First name prompt	To open the Text Box Properties dialog box. You'll label the form elements.
Edit the "Return data with this label" box to read **FirstName**	
Click **OK**	To close the Text Box Properties dialog box.
2 Double-click the textbox next to the Last name prompt	
3 Label the textbox **LastName**	Edit the "Return data with this label" box.
Click **OK**	
4 Assign unique names to the remaining textboxes	
5 Double-click the list box next to Country	To open the List Box Properties dialog box.
Label the list box **Country**	
Click **OK**	
6 Label the other list box **Publications**	
7 Double-click the checkbox next to Cooking	To open the Checkbox Properties dialog box.
Label the checkbox **Cooking**	
Click **OK**	
8 Label the checkbox next to Baking appropriately	

Tell students that their labels should logically correspond to the data they will pass, and that they should not contain spaces or punctuation.

9 Double-click the option button next to In printed form

To open the Option Button Properties dialog box. You want a user to be able to select only one option, so the label must be the same for both option buttons.

Label the option button **SendInfo**

Edit the Option button value box to read **Print**

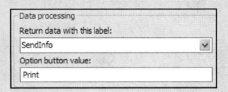

Click **OK**

10 Double-click the other option button

11 From the first list, select **SendInfo**

(Click the arrow to open the list.) To give it the same label as the other option button, making the two selections mutually exclusive.

Edit the Option button value box to read **Electronic**

Click **OK**

12 Label the Comments or questions text area **Comments**

13 Save the publication

Filling out a form

You can preview a form's behavior by previewing the publication in your Web browser. The form will behave as it would when it's published online, although you won't be able to submit the information until the page is uploaded and the server is configured to process the form data.

Do it!   ### B-3:   Previewing a form

Here's how	Here's why
1 Choose **File**, **Web Page Preview**	To open the form in your default Web browser.
Maximize the browser window	If necessary.
2 Complete the first column of the form with your personal information	
3 In the second column, check both **Cooking** and **Baking**	
4 In the list box, select **Newsletter**	
Press [CTRL]	
Select **Complete spice catalog**	To select all three options.
Release [CTRL]	
5 Select **In printed form**	
Select **Delivered electronically**	In printed form is deselected, because you can only select one option.
6 In the Comments or questions box, enter **Please send information about buying spices wholesale.**	
7 At the bottom of the page, click **Start over**	To clear the form.
8 Close the browser	To return to Publisher.
9 Save and close the publication	

It might take a minute to open the browser.

Tell students they might not need to complete the Address 2 field.

Tell students that, because they're not configured and connected to a Web server, submitting the form will return an error page in their browser.

Unit summary: Interactive forms

Topic A   In this topic, you learned about **Web forms**. You learned how to convert a print publication to a Web publication, and you learned how to use the **Web Tools toolbar** to insert **form elements**, including text areas, textboxes, list boxes, checkboxes, option buttons, and submit and reset buttons.

Topic B   In this topic, you learned how to **configure a form** to submit the data to an e-mail address, a database, or a processing program at your ISP. You learned about the importance of accurately and appropriately **labeling input fields**, and you learned the difference between creating checkbox labels and option button labels.

Independent practice activity

In this activity, you'll add form elements to a Web publication.

1 Open Practice form.pub (from the current unit folder).

2 Convert the publication to a Web publication, and save it as **My Practice form**.

3 Add textboxes for the First name, Last name, Email, Login name, and Password rows. Resize the textboxes to fill the column.

4 Give each textbox a unique label. Set the Password box to hide sensitive text with asterisks.

5 Add option buttons to the left of the Male and Female options. Give the option buttons the same label, so that selecting one clears the other; give each option button a unique value.

6 Insert a list box below the question "Where did you first hear of Outlander Spices?"

7 Add the following items to the list box: **Select one, Grocery store, Gourmet shop, The Web, A friend**.

8 Resize the list box so that only one option (Select one) appears.

9 Insert checkboxes before the choices **Online** and **In grocery stores**, and give each a unique label (so that a user could select one or both of the checkboxes).

10 Insert a text area in below Comments or questions, and widen it to fill the column.

11 At the bottom of the page, insert a submit button and make the button read **Send**.

12 Preview the form in your Web browser, and then close the browser.

13 Save and close My practice form.

Review questions

1 You're working on a publication and you want to use the Web Tools toolbar to insert form elements, but it isn't available in the View, Toolbars menu. Why not?

   To access the Web Tools toolbar, you must be working in a Web publication. Choose File, Convert to Web Publication to convert the file and access the Web Tools toolbar.

2 Explain the difference between a textbox and a text area.

   A textbox is used for short alphanumeric entries, usually on a single line. A text area allows long entries or multiple lines of text.

3 You've inserted a list box, but you want to format it so that only one option is visible and a user can click it to display the entire list. How do you do this?

   Resize the list box's height so that only one item appears. When a user clicks the list, it displays the entire list.

4 Explain the difference between checkboxes and option buttons.

   Checkboxes allow a user to select one or more items. Option buttons are usually grouped to allow only one selection, so that clicking one option button clears all the others in that group.

5 When you're creating a form that sends data to a database, the labels you choose for each input field must precisely match its corresponding field in the database. True or false?

   True

6 How should you label option boxes so that a user can only select one option from a group?

   Make the "Return data with this label" box the same for every option button that you want to include in a group. The Option button value box, however, should be unique for each option button.

U n i t 6

Web site publishing

Unit time: 45 minutes

Complete this unit, and you'll know how to:

A Check a Web publication for basic errors and omissions, add alternative text to a picture, create hyperlinks, and insert a navigation bar.

B Enter basic site information for search engines.

C Publish a Web site from within Publisher.

Topic A: Web elements

Explanation

When you're creating a Web publication, it's important that you check it for mistakes before you publish it. There are some important Web page elements that are commonly overlooked, particularly when converting a print publication to a Web publication, because a print publication does not require such things as hyperlinks between pages or a navigation bar. You can use the Design Checker to identify such errors and omissions in your Web publications.

Checking for basic errors and omissions

To check your Web publication for common mistakes, open the Design Checker pane and check "Run web site checks". The Design Checker will list any problems, as shown in Exhibit 6-1. If you check only "Run web site checks", Publisher looks for missing alternate text, which is important for users with alternative devices such as screen readers and Braille devices. It also checks to make sure that all the pages that will make up the Web site contain links so they can all be accessed. If you check both "Run web site checks" and "Run general design checks", Publisher will also look for basic content and layout mistakes, including:

- Overlapping elements
- Missing pictures
- Empty text boxes

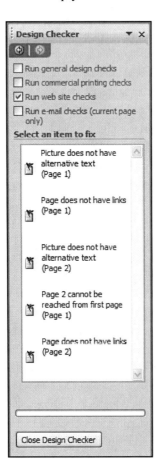

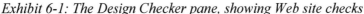

Exhibit 6-1: The Design Checker pane, showing Web site checks

Do it!

A-1:   Checking for basic Web site errors

Here's how	Here's why
1 Open About us.pub	(From the current unit folder.) This is a basic Web publication consisting of two pages. Each page in a publication appears as a separate Web page.
Save the publication as **My About us**	In the current unit folder.
2 Open the Design Checker pane	There are currently no problems listed in the Design Checker pane.
Check **Run web site checks**	You'll check for common Web site errors and omissions.
3 Read the results	

Tell students that this publication has already been converted to a Web publication.

Picture does not have alternative text (Page 1)

Page does not have links (Page 1)

Picture does not have alternative text (Page 2)

Page 2 cannot be reached from first page (Page 1)

Page does not have links (Page 2)

(In the "Select an item to fix" box.) There are several items that need to be fixed before you should publish it on the Web.

Alternative text

Explanation

Some people who visit your site might do so using an alternative browsing device such as a screen reader or Braille machine. Images are meaningless to these non-visual browsers, so it's important that you provide alternative text so that these users will have access to the content of the picture, or understand the picture's context in the page.

The alternative text you provide should depend on the nature of the picture. For example, if the image were the logo for Outlander Spices, a logical choice would be to indicate what the picture is, using alternative text that reads, "Outlander Spices logo." Also, if an image contains text, non-visual browsers can't read it, so it's important to use alternative text to duplicate the text in the image. If you have an image of a scene of some kind, or some other design-enhancing image, you might want to describe the scene in the image, or the purpose of the image.

To specify alternative text, open the Format Picture dialog box by selecting the picture and choosing Format, Picture. Activate the Web tab, and enter the appropriate text in the Alternative text box, as shown in Exhibit 6-2. You can also use the Design Checker pane to correct each item that appears in the list. To do so, point to an item in the "Select an item to fix" list, click the item's arrow, and select Fix: Add Alternative Text. The Format Picture dialog box opens with the Web tab activated.

Exhibit 6-2: The Web tab in the Format Picture dialog box

Do it!

A-2: Adding alternative text to a picture

Here's how	Here's why
1 Show the options for the first item	

Picture does not have alternative text (Page 1)

Go to this Item

Fix: Add Alternative Text...

Never Run this Check Again

Explain...

	Point to the item and click the arrow.
Select **Go to this Item**	(To make sure you know which page element the error is referencing.) The Outlander Spices logo on page 1 is selected.
2 Show the first item's options again	Point to the item and click the arrow.
Select **Fix: Add Alternative Text...**	To open the Format Picture dialog box. The Web tab is active.
In the Alternative text box, enter **Outlander Spices logo**	
Click **OK**	To close the dialog box. The item briefly appears with a green checkmark, and then disappears from the list.
3 Add alternative text to the logo on page 2	To provide alternative text to the other instance of the logo.
4 Save the publication	Next, you'll add hyperlinks so that users can navigate between the pages.

Tell them to enter the same alternative text as the first instance of the logo.

Hyperlinks

Explanation

A *hyperlink*, or *link* for short, is text or an image that connects to another page, another location on the same page, another site, or some other resource when a user clicks it. When you point to a hyperlink in Publisher, a ScreenTip appears. By default, hyperlinks are blue and underlined, but you can change their appearance to fit your color scheme.

Inserting hyperlinks in a publication

You can use hyperlinks to link to an existing file or Web page or to another place in the same document. You also can use hyperlinks to create a new document or to send an e-mail. To link to another place in the same document, you first need to insert bookmarks, and then link to those bookmarks.

To insert a hyperlink in a publication:

1   Select the text that you want to make a hyperlink.

2   On the Web Tools toolbar, click the Insert Hyperlink button, or press Ctrl+K to open the Insert Hyperlink dialog box, shown in Exhibit 6-3.

3   Under Link to, select an option:

- **Existing File or Web Page**—Use this option to link to an existing file, such as a Word document or Excel spreadsheet.

- **Place in This Document**—Use this option to link to a specific page, a bookmark, or the first, last, next, or previous page in the publication.

- **Create New Document**—Use this option to create a new publication in a specific location on your computer and with a name that you choose.

- **E-mail Address**—Use this option to create a new e-mail, addressed to an e-mail address and, optionally, a subject line that you specify.

4   Click OK.

Some of these hyperlink options are suitable only for viewing a publication on screen. For example, you wouldn't create a hyperlink on a page that opens an Excel spreadsheet on your computer and then publish the page to the Web. Likewise, you wouldn't use a hyperlink to create a new document if the page is intended for the Web. Instead, these kinds of links are useful for viewing pages offline; for example, your publication might include links to a list of spreadsheets that you want to be able to locate quickly.

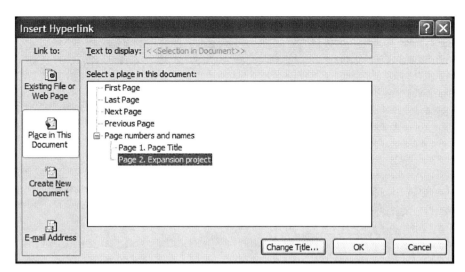

Exhibit 6-3: The Insert Hyperlink dialog box

Using hyperlinks

In Publisher, simply clicking a hyperlink does not activate it like it does in a Web browser. To use a hyperlink in Publisher, press and hold Ctrl, and then click the link. If a link points to an external file, the linked file will open in its source application, if available.

Do it!

A-3: Creating a hyperlink

Here's how	Here's why
1 Observe the first item to be fixed	(In the Design Checker pane.) The first item in the list is now "Page does not have links". This error is present on both page 1 and page 2. While it's not an absolute requirement for every Web page to contain links, a page without any links is isolated from the flowing, interrelated structure of a typical Web site.
2 Scroll to the bottom of page 1 and zoom to 100%	(If necessary.) You'll create a hyperlink that will jump to page 2.
3 Select the text shown	**About our future** Read about our expansion project.
4 On the Web Tools toolbar, click [icon]	(The Insert Hyperlink button.). To open the Insert Hyperlink dialog box.
Under Link to, select **Place in This Document**	

5 Select **Page 2. Page Title**	First Page
	Last Page
	Next Page
	Previous Page
	Page numbers and names
	   Page 1. Page Title
	   Page 2. Page Title

Click **Change Title**	To open the Enter Text dialog box.
Type **Expansion project**	
Click **OK**	To close the dialog box.
Click **OK**	To close the Insert Hyperlink dialog box.
6 Observe the text	The text is blue and underlined to indicate that it's a hyperlink. (You can change the default hyperlink styles to fit your site's color scheme.)

TIPS ✓ *Tell students they can also press Ctrl+K.*

7 Press and hold CTRL

Point to the link

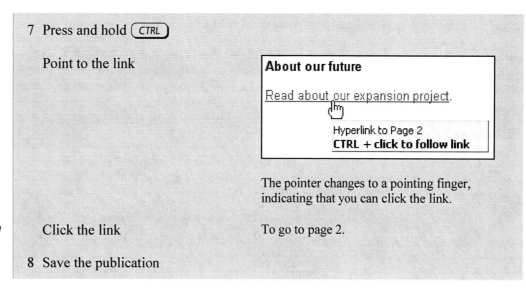

Tell them they might have to scroll up to view the page content.

The pointer changes to a pointing finger, indicating that you can click the link.

Click the link

To go to page 2.

8 Save the publication

Navigation bars

Explanation

A *navigation bar* shows the major pages or sections of a Web site and contains links to them so that a user can navigate to any page from any other page in the site. In Publisher, you can create a navigation bar that automatically creates links for every page in your publication. You can also customize the style, size, and orientation of the navigation bar by selecting options in the Design Gallery dialog box, shown in Exhibit 6-4. To insert a navigation bar:

1 On the Web Tools toolbar, click the Navigation Bar button to open the Design Gallery dialog box with the Navigation Bars section active.

2 Select the desired style.

3 In the rightmost pane of the dialog box, select an orientation.

4 Under Apply a design, select a size for the buttons on the navigation bar, or select Text only.

5 Clear Show selected state if you don't want the active page's corresponding button to indicate that a user is currently viewing that page.

6 Under Insert options, select whether to insert a navigation bar on each existing page, or to insert it on only the current page.

7 Click Insert Object.

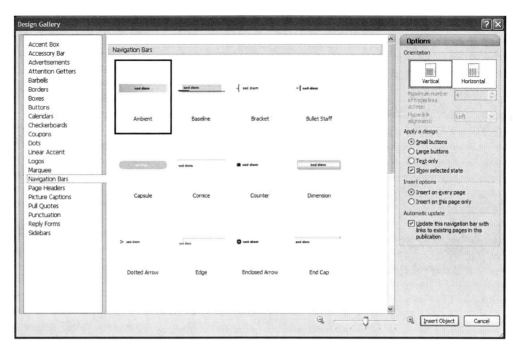

Exhibit 6-4: Navigation bar options in the Design Gallery dialog box

After you've created a navigation bar, you can move it to a desired location in the layout. You can also edit the name of each link and change the formatting, as necessary. If you edit the text in a link on one page, the change will be reflected in the corresponding links on all other pages—if you've inserted a navigation bar on more than one page. However, formatting changes that you make will apply only to the current page.

A-4: Inserting a navigation bar

Here's how	Here's why
1 Scroll to the top of page 1	You'll insert a navigation bar so that users can navigate each page.
2 On the Web Tools toolbar, click [icon]	(The Navigation Bar button.) To open the Design Gallery dialog box; the Navigation Bars section is active.
3 Select **Bullet Staff**	The fourth option in the first row.
4 Observe the Options section	You can choose between a vertical or horizontal navigation bar. You also can use small or large buttons or show text only. Because "Show selected state" is selected, the button that links to the active page will use a different color. By default, Publisher inserts a navigation bar on every page in the publication, and it updates the navigation bar when you add or remove pages to the publication.
Click **Insert Object**	The navigation bar appears in the middle of the page. You'll need to move it to the desired location in the layout. The button for the first page uses the default page title, but you've changed the title for the second page.
5 Drag the navigation bar to the area shown	
6 Select the text shown	
	This is the default text that Publisher applies when a page does not have a title.
Type **About us**	To specify a title for the page and create a link to it.

The navigation bar is duplicated on as many pages as the Web site contains.

7 Go to page 2

Publisher created a duplicate navigation bar for page 2. When you edited the text in the navigation bar on page 1, Publisher automatically updated the corresponding text in this instance of the navigation bar.

Tell students that it doesn't have to be in the precise location as the first navigation bar, but in their actual Web pages, they should make it as exact as possible.

8 Place the navigation bar as shown

Notice that the bullet appears next to the second link in this instance of the navigation bar, reinforcing the currently active page.

9 Preview the publication in your default Web browser

Choose File, Web Page Preview.

10 Click **About us**

To follow the link.

11 Click **Expansion project**

To navigate to the other page.

12 Close the browser

To return to Publisher.

13 Observe the Design Checker pane

There are no more errors listed.

Save the publication

Topic B: Web page options

Explanation

Before you publish a site on the Web, you should establish a naming convention for the pages and content resources in your site. In addition, you can increase the likelihood that search engine users will find your site by specifying keywords relevant to the content and purpose of your site. You can apply these settings by using the Web Page Options dialog box.

The Web Page Options dialog box

On the Web Tools toolbar, click the Web Page Options button to open the Web Page Options dialog box, shown in Exhibit 6-5. The following table describes the options available in this dialog box.

Option	Description
Page title	When a user views a Web page, its title appears in the title bar of the browser. Page titles are also critical to successful search engine results. Many search engines use the page title as the link to a page in a list of search results. Without a title, a search engine will have to use the first text that appears on the page, which might not make sense out of context.
File name	By default, a Web site's homepage uses the filename "index.htm." For example, if a user entered "outlanderspices.com" in a Web browser, the browser would navigate to "outlanderspices.com/index.htm." Publisher names the first page in a Web publication "index.htm" by default. But subsequent pages get automatically generated names. If you want to use your own file names, such as "products.htm," enter it in the File name box.
Search engine information	Enter a brief description of your site and keywords that are relevant to your site's content and purpose, so that users might find your site when they enter those keywords in a search engine.
Background sound	If you want music to play when a user views a particular page, you can add it by clicking Browse under Background sound. Keep in mind, however, that this might make your page take longer to load, and some users consider background music unnecessary and annoying.

Exhibit 6-5: The Web Page Options dialog box

Do it!

B-1:   Entering information for search engines

Here's how	Here's why
1 Go to page 1	If necessary.
2 On the Web Tools toolbar, click ![button]	(The Web Page Options button.) To open the Web Page Options dialog box.
3 Type **About us**	To specify a title for this page.
4 In the Description box, type **Outlander Spices is the leading supplier of high-quality spices from all over the world.**	
5 In the Keywords box, enter **outlander, spices, cooking, recipes, cuisine**	
Click **OK**	To close the dialog box.
6 Save the publication	

Point out that this is just a simple example of a list of keywords, and does not represent an exhaustive list.

Topic C: Web site publishing

Explanation

When you convert a publication to a Web publication, it's still a Publisher file. To make it accessible on the Web, it must be converted to HTML format, which happens automatically when you publish a site from within Publisher. You also need to upload the files to a public server so that users can access them. A network server can be local, such as your company's intranet, or a World Wide Web server.

Publishing a Web site

To publish a Web site, choose File, Publish to the Web to open the Publish to the Web dialog box. From here, you have several options for publishing your site—you can publish a Web site to a location on the Internet or on a network, you can publish a Web site using FTP, or you can save a Web site to a folder on your computer.

Saving a Web site to your computer

To save a Web site to a folder on your computer, open the Publish to the Web dialog box. Then, navigate to the desired location and click Save, as you would when saving a Publisher file. Publisher converts the site to HTML, saves the index page to the indicated location, and also creates a folder for any other pages in the site as well as any graphics included in the site.

File Transfer Protocol (FTP)

File Transfer Protocol is the most commonly used method for uploading Web site files to a network server. *FTP* was designed specifically for copying large numbers of files from one location to another.

To publish a Web site using FTP:

1 In the Publish to the Web dialog box, from the Save in list, select Add/Modify FTP Locations. The Add/Modify FTP Locations dialog box opens.
2 In the Name of FTP site dialog box, enter the URL of your site.
3 Select User, and enter your user name.
4 In the Password box, enter your password.
5 Click OK to close the dialog box and add the FTP location to the Save in list.
6 Select the FTP location, and click Open. The site directory appears.
7 If necessary, navigate to the desired location in your site by double-clicking the folders. (The index.htm file should be saved in the root directory—for example, ftp://outlanderspices.com/. However, in some cases, the root directory might be a folder named "html," for example.)
8 Click Save to upload the site.

Exhibit 6-6: The Add/Modify FTP Locations dialog box

Do it!

C-1: Publishing a Web site

Here's how	Here's why
1 On the Web Tools toolbar, click	(The Publish to the Web button.) You'll publish this two-page Web site, which will automatically convert the publication to HTML format.
Read the alert dialog box	The dialog box indicates that you need a Web hosting provider to publish your Web site. You can also publish a Web site to a location on your local computer, and upload the converted files at a later date.
Click **OK**	The Publish to the Web dialog box opens.
2 In the Save in list, navigate to the current unit folder	
Click the Create New Folder button, as shown	
	You'll create a folder to publish the Web site into.
In the Name box, enter **Web site** and click **OK**	
3 Observe the File name box	By default, Publisher saves the first page as index.htm. You can change this default file name if necessary.
Click **Save**	An alert dialog box appears, providing information about the nature of the publication and how you can modify it if necessary.
Click **OK**	
4 Save and close the publication	
5 In Windows Explorer, navigate to the Web site folder	In the current unit folder.
Observe the converted HTML file and folder	Publisher converted both pages to HTML files. The index.htm page is saved in the root folder, which in this case is the current unit folder. This acts as the home page. Publisher also created a folder named index_files, which contains the other HTML page and all the required images and other resources.
6 Close Windows Explorer	

TIPS Tell students they can also choose File, Publish to the Web.

Tell students that, in their own projects, they should make page 1 in a publication be the intended home page, which Publisher will save as index.htm.

Unit summary: Web site publishing

Topic A

In this topic, you learned how to use the **Design Checker** to check for basic Web site errors and omissions, and you learned how to specify **alternative text** for images. Then you learned how to create **hyperlinks**, and use them within Publisher. Finally, you learned how to create and modify **navigation bars**.

Topic B

In this topic, you learned how to specify a site **description**, and you applied a list of relevant **keywords** to help optimize a Web site for search engine users.

Topic C

In this topic, you learned how to **publish a Web site** from within Publisher. You learned that Publisher automatically converts a publication to HTML when you use the Publish to the Web dialog box. You also learned how to **add an FTP location**.

Independent practice activity

In this activity, you'll open an existing Web publication, apply alternative text to a series of images, create a navigation bar, and publish the Web site in the current unit folder.

1   Open Product Section.pub (from the current unit folder). This four-page file has already been converted to a Web publication.

2   Save the file as **My Product Section**.

3   On page 1, specify appropriate alternative text for the bay leaf image. (*Hint*: Right-click the Bay leaf image and choose Format, Picture. Activate the Web tab, and enter your alternative text.)

4   Specify alternative text for the images on pages 2-4.

5   Create a navigation bar using the Bracket style. (*Hint*: On the Web Tools toolbar, click the Navigation Bar button. In the Design Gallery, select Bracket, and click Insert Object.)

6   On each page, drag the navigation bar to the upper left corner of each page, as shown in Exhibit 6-7.

7   Edit the default "Page Title" text for each link as shown in Exhibit 6-8.

8   Preview the page in your default Web browser, test the links on all four pages, and then close the browser.

9   Publish the Web site into a new folder in the current unit folder. Name the new folder Practice site.

10 Save and close the publication.

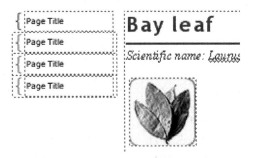

Exhibit 6-7: The navigation bar on page 1

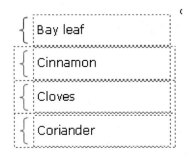

Exhibit 6-8: The navigation bar, after completing step 7

Review questions

1 If you upload a Publisher file (a .pub file) directly to the Web, will users be able to open the file in a Web browser?

   No. You need to publish it from within Publisher, which converts the publication to HTML.

2 Where should the index.htm file be saved?

   In the root directory

3 When you have an image in a Web page that contains text, what should your alternative text for that image be?

   The alternative text should duplicate the text in the image.

4 If you have an image in a Web page of a sunset over a lake, which is intended solely as a design component, what should your alternative text for that image be?

   The alternative text should describe the image to provide users with non-visual browsers some idea of the image's purpose or context within the page.

5 How can you test a hyperlink while viewing a publication in Publisher?

   Press and hold Ctrl, and then click the link.

6 What is the default file name for a Web site's home page?

   The default name is index.htm.

7 How do you add an FTP location in Publisher?

   Choose File, Publish to the Web. From the Save in list, select Add/Modify FTP Locations (or select an existing location). Navigate to the desired folder, and then click Save.

Course summary

This summary contains information to help you bring the course to a successful conclusion. Using this information, you will be able to:

A Use the summary text to reinforce what students have learned in class.

B Direct students to the next courses in this series (if any), and to any other resources that might help students continue to learn about Microsoft Publisher 2007.

Topic A: Course summary

At the end of the class, use the following summary text to reinforce what students have learned. It is intended not as a script, but rather as a starting point.

Unit summaries

Unit 1

In this unit, students learned how to create a brochure layout. They also learned how to create a **business information set**, change a publication's **color scheme**, and apply **tint swatches** and **gradients**. Then students learned how to use the **Content Library**. Finally, they learned how to link an embedded picture and replace a picture.

Unit 2

In this unit, students learned how to work with **styles**. They learned how to apply a **font scheme**, work with **WordArt** objects, and create a **type mask**. They also learned how to adjust **text wrap** to wrap to an image's contours, snap text to a **baseline guide**, and **distribute text horizontally**. Finally, students learned how to insert **symbols** and **special characters**.

Unit 3

In this unit, students learned how to create **sections** in a publication. They also learned how to apply **page numbers** for separate sections, add **bookmarks**, and navigate to bookmarks.

Unit 4

In this unit, students learned how to create a **recipient list** for a mail merge. They also created a publication using a **label template** in order to prepare it for a mail merge. Then students began a mail merge by using the Mail Merge pane and **sorted** and **filtered** the recipient list. Finally, they learned how to add **mail merge fields** to a publication and then complete a mail merge by creating a **merged publication**.

Unit 5

In this unit, students learned how to create a Web publication. They learned how to use the Web Tools toolbar to create a **form** and insert **input fields**. They also learned how to set **form properties** and label input fields.

Unit 6

In this unit, students learned how to preview a Web publication and **convert a print publication to a Web publication**. They also learned how to check a Web site for typical errors and omissions, apply **alternative text** to images, create **hyperlinks**, and insert a **navigation bar**. Finally, students learned how to enter a **site description** and **keywords** for search engine indexing, and **publish a Web site** from within Publisher.

Topic B: Continued learning after class

Point out to your students that it is impossible to learn to use any software effectively in a single day. To get the most out of this class, students should begin working with Publisher 2007 to perform real tasks as soon as possible. Course Technology also offers resources for continued learning.

Next courses in this series

This is the last course in this series.

Other resources

For more information, visit www.course.com.

Publisher 2007: Advanced

Quick reference

Button	Shortcut keys	Function
	CTRL + W	Closes a publication.
		Inserts WordArt.
		Opens the WordArt Gallery dialog box.
		Opens the Format WordArt dialog box.
		Displays a list of WordArt shapes.
		Aligns WordArt.
		Adjust the letter height of WordArt.
		Opens the Bookmark dialog box.
		Opens the Publish to the Web dialog box.
		Opens the Web page in your default browser.
	CTRL + K	When text or a picture is selected, opens the Insert Hyperlink dialog box.
		Changes the cursor to a crosshair, which you can drag to create a hot spot; a *hot spot* is an area on the page that acts as a hyperlink.
		Opens the Design Gallery dialog box, with the Navigation Bars section active.
		Opens the Web Page Options dialog box and automatically selects the current page title so that you can edit it.
		Opens the Background task pane.

Button	Function
	Opens the Web Page Options dialog box, which you can use to insert a background sound (for example, a music file) on your Web page.
	Displays a list of options for inserting form elements.
	Opens the Edit HTML Code Fragment dialog box.
	Opens the Options dialog box, with the Web tab active.
	Opens the Web Page Options dialog box.

Glossary

Accordion fold

A common method for folding a brochure so that each column on a page becomes a panel in the brochure, which folds out like an accordion.

Baseline guides

A set of non-printing lines that run along the width of a publication page to align columns of text.

Bookmark

A marker that marks a location in a publication, which you can then navigate to directly by clicking the associated bookmark entry in the Bookmark dialog box.

Business information set

A set of information about you and your company stored in Publisher.

Checkbox

A form component that allows a user to select one or more items from a group of items.

Color scheme

The set of default colors that appear in the Fill Color, Line Color, and Font Color palettes.

Content Library

A task pane that stores items such as text, graphics, or shapes independently of all publications, so that you can access the items at any time regardless of what you are working on.

Em dash

The character that typically is meant by "dash"—a strong break (such as this one) in the flow of a sentence—and longer than either a hyphen or an en dash.

En dash

A character typically used in place of "through," such as in "pages 3–15," and that is longer than a hyphen but shorter than an em dash.

Embedded picture

A picture included in the publication, rather than linked to it.

Font scheme

A set that includes a heading and a body font.

FTP (File Transfer Protocol)

A system designed specifically for copying a large number of files and files that are large in size from one location to another over a network.

Gradient

A blend of one or more colors, in which the colors appear along a spectrum with the colors blending where they meet.

HTML (Hypertext Markup Language)

A standard markup language that allows you to display text, images, and multimedia files on the Web.

Hyperlink

Text or an image that connects to another page, another location on the same page, another site, or some other resource when you click it.

Hyphen

A character typically used to combine compound words, and that is shorter than an en dash or an em dash.

Link

See *hyperlink*.

Linked picture

A picture saved separately from the publication—a low-resolution preview of the picture appears in the publication, but it isn't included with the publication.

List box

A form component that allows a user to select one or more items from a list.

Navigation bar

A Web page component that lists the pages available in a Web site and contains links to them so that a user can navigate to any one page from any page in the site.

Option button

A form component that allows users to select one item from a group of items. Clicking one option button clears all the others in that group.

Recipient list

A list of names and addresses stored in an external file that can be used in Publisher to complete a mail merge.

Section

A portion of a publication in which you can set the page number formatting separately from the rest of the publication.

Shade

The percentage of black mixed with an ink.

Styles

Named sets of formatting options that define the appearance of recurring text components, such as headings or body text.

Submit button

In a form, a button usually linked to a script that transmits the field values from the form to the database or Web server where the information is to be processed.

Text area

In a form, allows long entries or multiple lines of text.

Textbox

A form component used for short alphanumeric entries, usually on a single line.

Tint

The percentage of white mixed with an ink.

Type mask

A technique wherein an image appears only in the letters of some text.

Index

B

Baseline guides, 2-24
Bookmarks
    Adding, 3-6
    Deleting, 3-8
    Locating, 3-8
Brochures
    Setting up, 1-4
Business information sets, 1-7

C

Checkboxes, 5-10
Colors
    Custom, 1-11
Content Library, 1-18
    Using the, 1-21

E

Error checking, 6-2

F

Fonts
    Schemes for, 2-12
Forms
    Labels for, 5-16
    Properties of, 5-14
FTP, 6-16

G

Gradients, 1-16
Graphics Manager, 1-23

H

Hyperlinks, 6-6

L

List boxes, 5-7

M

Mail Merge pane, 4-6
Mailing labels, 4-5
Merge fields, 4-11
    Modifying, 4-12

N

Navigation bars, 6-10

O

Option buttons, 5-10

P

Pictures
    Embedded, 1-24
    Linked, 1-24
    Replacing, 1-26
Publications
    Merged, 4-14

R

Recipient lists, 4-2
    Attaching, 4-6
Records
    Filtering, 4-10
    Sorting, 4-8

S

Sections
    Creating, 3-2
    Paginating, 3-4
Shades, 1-14
Special characters, 2-31
Styles, 2-2
    Applying, 2-10
    Creating, 2-6
    Overriding, 2-11
    Using existing, 2-8
Submit buttons, 5-11
Symbols, 2-29

T

Templates, 1-2
Text
    Alternative, 6-4
    Contour-based wraps for, 2-22
    Horizontal distribution of, 2-28
Textboxes, 5-5
Tints, 1-14
Type masks, 2-18

W

Web elements, 6-2
Web forms, 5-2

Web Page options, 6-14
Web sites
  Publishing, 6-16
WordArt, 2-14